Shooting The List

THE FILMMAKER'S ART VOL. 3

Markus Innocenti

RED DOG LOGIC

LOS ANGELES, CALIFORNIA

Book Layout & Design ©2013 — BookDesignTemplates.com
Cover Design — Red Dog Logic
Front Cover Photo from the Everett Collection, licensed through Shutterstock
Images from The Missing Link used with permission

Published by Red Dog Logic, an imprint of
Park Circle Limited, Glasgow, Scotland UK

ISBN 978-0-9986364-4-3

FOREWORD

Most Screenwriters and Film Directors are people you've never heard of.

The famous ones, past and present, have always been the tip of a very large iceberg. Of those who do manage to make a regular living as a key creative, most remain anonymous to all but their immediate family and colleagues. A few of us don't even try to break the surface and become 'known' — but ego being what it is, those willing to toil without caring whether they are ever recognized or not are the exception.

I'm no different from most. After 35 years in the business, I'm still trying to write, direct or produce a film that — when I mention its title — most people will go, '*Oh, yeah, I saw that*'. So far, only my music videos have that distinction — but I'm still working on it. It's been a fun journey, even if the limo rides have been few and far between.

A while back I started thinking about what I've learned in my career. You get to the point where you want to pass something on, usually because what you're seeing, and hearing, is making you slap your own forehead too many times a day.

Let me share a secret. A few days before I directed my first full-length theatrical feature film, I realized that I'd never done this before and I wasn't sure how I was going to get through the 30-day shoot. I had no real idea how to go about making a fiction drama. I was an experienced music video director, I'd made a couple of well-received 'shorts', produced a documentary, and I'd directed some commercials. On the basis of that, the executives and the agents and the star actors figured I knew what I was doing. I was in the solitary position of knowing that when it came to direct a theatrical feature — I didn't have a clue.

Nowadays, there's so much information on filmmaking, in particular on screenwriting and directing, you begin to wonder who's buying all these books and attending all those seminars. When I started out, there was nothing except William Goldman's entertainingly brilliant *Adventures in the Screen Trade* and *Truffaut/Hitchcock* — Francois Truffaut's massive interview with Sir Alfred. Other than that, you just had to figure it out from watching other people's work and trusting that you had a 'vision'.

So how did I get to this position of having producers, agents and stars believe that my business partner and creative collaborator, Edward Arno, and I were ready to take the leap into making what the contract specified as a 'First Class International Theatrical Feature Film'?

I'd been an actor for a while, but when people ask how I got started I tell them I entered the film industry in a truck — which is true. I had a job delivering grip equipment from rental houses to film sets. Most deliveries were for television commercial productions, but a few were for the big features. I had an epiphany one day after I'd brought some camera support equipment to Pinewood (a major studio outside London, England). I wandered onto the *Superman* (1978) set, the movie that made Christopher Reeve famous. I couldn't get over the size of the New York street exterior set — a massive façade for the 'Daily Planet' building where 'Clark Kent' and 'Lois Lane' worked. Looking at the activity, I began to understand more fully how the magic of film was mostly smoke, mirrors and a lot of painted plywood. I guess I got fired up because within five years I co-owned a stage and film production design company and was a union-accredited Art Director.

Everything in the film business is a small-step-by-small-step progress. There are seldom instant leaps. Eight years after that day on the *Superman* set, I was a music video director. Two years after that, and I was represented by one of the big agencies and signed to co-direct my first theatrical feature. And so there I was, just a few days before Principal Photography was due to begin, nervously realizing I hadn't actually directed a major long-form dramatic work before.

Most people who are even halfway good at anything tend to forget how hard and long the journey has been and how prepared they really are when the moment of truth arrives. They often think their success has been a fluke and that at any moment someone will pull back the curtain and expose their lack of talent. I was no exception. Gripped by a full-blown case of Imposter Syndrome I began to panic — until I remembered one of the first rules of success. If you don't know — ask. Even if, in asking, you risk making yourself look ridiculous.

I called author Steven Bernstein who'd recently completed what would become the best-selling *Film Production* (a standard student text from the moment it was published by Focal Press). Steven (who was on his way to becoming one of Hollywood's A-list Cinematographers and a Director in his own right) took ten minutes out of his day, told me to take a deep breath, reminded me that I'd already directed thousands of set-ups, and then proceeded to give me a step-by-step method of how to walk onto a feature film set and make it look as if I knew what I was doing.
Steven Bernstein's generous insights gave me the knowledge and confidence to get through the first few hours on my debut feature without looking like a complete idiot, and since then I've built on that beginning.

Becoming a film director is no different from the learning curves and progressions made by artists working in any other of the creative arts or crafts. You start off a little unsure, a little hesitant and perhaps much too rigid in your own self-belief. Gradually, you learn how to do things the way they most often get done, you start to solve problems in ways that other artists have solved those problems before, and you feel your way towards the results you're looking for — most often with a large sense of dissatisfaction. Over time, like an improvisational jazz musician, you become so accustomed to your 'craft' and so adept at achieving your goal that you are able to apply your 'art' — the thing that distinguishes you from the others. The rules and rigidity no longer seem so necessary — but they are there to fall back on, the way a jazz musician knows the key, the mode and the scale that the musical structure relies upon.

The Filmmaker's Art series is designed to give you detailed basic knowledge that will allow you to step onto any movie set in the world and direct. From those essential basics — which every aspiring film-maker thinks they know, but actually don't — you will establish an acceptable 'craft' and a solid jumping-off point to start creating your own 'art'.

As I go through the series, I'll be looking to take you beyond the basics so that you can develop your own signature style. Bear in mind that my goal is to take you from 'craft' to 'art' in a business where 'art' often doesn't seem to count for very much — but is completely present in the work of the masters.

This book follows on from *Decoding The Script* and *Selecting For Success*. *Decoding The Script* discussed how Directors read scripts in ways that nobody else does, and how they identify elements within the script that will be overlooked by most readers, but which are vital to directing a film. *Selecting for Success* focused on how Directors organize those elements and bring the script they have decoded into film production.

Shooting The List is the third step, and the last book in the series to discuss issues present in the Development and Pre-Production phases.

If you're already on your film-making journey, or even if you've yet to begin, some of what follows may seem obvious and already acquired. I hope you'll take a moment to allow those parts which might seem familiar to soak in completely and perhaps be reassessed.

Because even the greatest musicians sit down and practice scales now and again.

The Best Train-Set A Boy Ever Had.

—ORSON WELLES

CHAPTER ONE

What's The Big Deal?

I read recently, and with some amazement, that a Shot List is now considered 'old school' and people are making films without one.

Alright, so maybe I'm not amazed. Today's filmmakers are so steeped in visual storytelling that techniques which would have been hard to access and understand for previous generations of emerging directors are now second nature. If you grow up with a screen in your hand, and constant exposure to visual imagery — much of it striking and fresh — then the primary elements of film technique are hard-wired into you in the same way that children learn their native language. Perhaps that is my point — the point of this book. You might be able to speak a language fluently, but you may not have an insight and understanding of how the various elements of that language are formed and how they operate. In short, the use and command of language is 'instinctive' and to a large degree 'rote-learned' and 'habitual'. It has been learned by listening to (or watching) others repeatedly and copying what has been heard (or seen) until fluency and comprehension is achieved.

This would seem to be the one of several reasons why the Shot List is disappearing from the film sets of many young and emerging directors. Technology is another. Why would you need a Shot List when you can simply scroll through your captured media and check that you have everything you require? With a 'Video Village' on-set — or a complete Edit Suite on your laptop — you can look at, even rough edit-assemble, your work within minutes of shooting a scene.

So, is this book redundant before it has begun? Maybe, but I hope you will indulge me. My argument for devoting an entire volume of *The Filmmaker's Art* to the subject of The Shot List is because I'd like you to fully consider the elements of film story-telling. To lift the hood and look at the moving parts. To understand the 'grammar'. I'm going to try and make the case for The Shot List as briefly as I can and, perhaps, clear up for you any aspects of the 'grammar' that haven't been immediately apparent to you despite the fact that you already may have a 'fluency' that you and your colleagues and collaborators have confidence in.

Sometimes, having a basic Shot List in your hand is purely for the comfort of others…

I visited an 'indie' film set recently, where an emerging Director was laboring to bring his 'vision' into reality. A couple of the Actors recognized me and came over to say 'hello'.
'How's it going?' I asked.
'He doesn't have a Shot List,' they replied, each one with a slightly scared and helpless look in their eyes.

Now, it wasn't that the Actors I spoke to were wimps and lost little lambs. These were toughened professionals who'd worked on some of the biggest movies you could name. What scared them, and made them feel helpless, was that they'd put themselves in the hands of a novice Director who — because he didn't appear to have a Shot List — would perhaps not get the 'coverage' he needed to properly edit the scenes, potentially leaving them looking bad.

Actors cannot be blamed for worrying that all the hard work of their preparation and performance is not being 'covered' well enough to allow an editor to carve out a great scene. That's why they're always surprised when you've shot the scene out. They're usually ready to do some more. It's sometimes necessary to allay those fears and tell them that you have all the material you need.

And seeing as we've mentioned this word 'Coverage', let me explain what it means because you're going to be asked endlessly by producers if you've got the 'Coverage' you want, or simply if you are 'Covered'.

Think of 'Coverage' as shooting a series of shots that will allow you to edit the scene any way you like. Think also of 'Coverage' as a safety net that will allow an editor to choose a different shot if something isn't working. Note that doesn't mean a different 'take' — although, in a sense, multiple takes give you 'safety' also.

'Coverage' traditionally means first doing a 'Master' Shot that runs through the entire scene, from either a fixed position, or with camera movement. The Master Shot shows everything that is going on in the scene, so generally it is a 'Wide' shot. The terms are sometimes interchangeable. *"Did you get a 'Master'?/Did you shoot a 'Wide'?"* Then come (usually) closer or 'tighter' shots that 'cover' the same action, often of the entire scene but more usually snippets or short sequences of that scene. These shots can then be edited with the Master to create a sequence that moves and has pace, and which allows the editor to trim out unnecessary moments, re-arrange the order of the sequence, and extend or compress 'Time'.

Most importantly, in terms of how we understand 'Coverage', the various shots free up the editor to assemble a scene without being forced into using material that is technically or creatively flawed.

Let's imagine that you are filming an actor performing Hamlet's *'To be or not to be'* soliloquy from Bill Shakespeare's eponymous play. Depending on the level of carpet-chewing, the 33 lines of dialogue will run from two to four minutes. In olden times, before the miracle of digital, if you shot a MASTER of your Actor delivering the lines, followed that with 3 takes of a CLOSE-UP of the performance, and then called a 'wrap' — you'd better hope that the negative would come back from the lab in pristine condition, without scratches or dirt and — vitally — in focus.

In our bright, shiny modern times, scratched negative is no longer a concern unless we are one of the world's top filmmakers and have a budget, a quality concern, and distribution model that requires the disappearing technology. Even in those circumstances, film can be made pristine by digital means — the problem 'painted out'. But other problems can arise to kick we lesser mortals of the digerati in the butt. Because if the MASTER in our example is unusable at a certain point, and all three takes of the CLOSE-UP have a poor performance or dialogue stumble or any number of problems *at that same exact moment* – then, what is our editor going to do? There's always a solution of course, but with minimal footage the choices you make to 'save the edit' are going to be harsh and uncomfortable. If you'd 'covered' this simple monologue better, you'd be safe. There would have been another shot, another angle that would have replaced the NG ('no-good') Footage. Your Producer would have breathed a sigh of relief and patted you on the back for your 'professionalism'.

Proper 'Coverage' in our *Hamlet's Soliloquy* example might be; (1) The Master. (2) A Medium Shot. (3) A Close Up. (4) An Extreme Close Up – Lips/Mouth, Eyes, Hands. (5) A Cutaway (in this case perhaps a shot of an inanimate object — a portrait, a vase of flowers, Poor Yorick's skull — although, come to think of it, that's a prop from a different scene!).

To get two opposing views of this matter, I point you to the Soliloquy performances in two greatly different film versions. Franco Zeffirelli's *Hamlet* (1990), with Mel Gibson in the title role, has 14 different shots used for the scene (there may have been more that didn't make it into the edit). They include WIDE, LONG SHOT, MEDIUM, MEDIUM CLOSE UP, CLOSE-UP, LO-ANGLE MEDIUM CLOSE-UP and CUTAWAY.

Kenneth Branagh' s *Hamlet* (1996) (with Branagh in the role) on the other hand, has what is essentially a SINGLE shot, with the exception of a fast CUTAWAY (to Derek Jacobi as 'Claudius') which could be described as a 'REACTION' shot. But Branagh's masterly SINGLE is, in truth, a multitude of shots, as he TRUCKS the camera from a position behind his shoulder (OTS) towards a reflection of himself in a full-length mirror. One shot — but it goes from FULL to CLOSE-UP.

Let's briefly discuss these two versions for a moment, as they relate to 'Coverage'. You don't have to have seen either sequence to understand my points but — like everything else — they are available on You Tube.

The '*To be or not to be*' soliloquy from Shakespeare's *Hamlet* is one of the best known and most revered speeches in the English language. It is so familiar that it is something of a litmus test of an Actor's skills. For his Soliloquy Sequence, Zeffirelli shot at least 14 Set-ups, some obviously requiring more 'takes' than others. It would have been a lengthy day (or days) with much repositioning of camera and lighting. Clearly, 14 shots of various sizes would have given him many possibilities in the edit and that alone might have been reason enough for an extensive Shot List. With that many shots at his disposal, he could choose to increase or decrease tension and pace. He could manipulate mood, emotion and the audience's understanding and involvement. But there's something else.

Given that Zeffirelli was a highly-experienced and sensitive filmmaker, who had already had a popular, mainstream success with his version of Shakespeare's *Romeo & Juliet* (1968), I'd suggest that he wanted to give Mel Gibson the best opportunity for a positive critical outcome. At the time, before becoming a Director himself, Mr. Gibson was a celebrated Action-Adventure Star, best known for *Lethal Weapon* (1987). You can imagine the raised eyebrows when it was announced that 'Mad Max' was going to play the quintessential Shakespearean role. Zeffirelli and Mr. Gibson would have known that to perform this particular monologue would open them to scrutiny, a scrutiny that perhaps would not be charitable and might even elicit scorn. So, what do you do in those circumstances? You carefully create an imaginative Shot List, no doubt backed up with a Storyboard, and you 'cover' the heck out of the scene.

You make it popular, mainstream 'cinema'.

When he came to direct and star in his screen version of *Hamlet*, Kenneth Branagh was already a highly-regarded Shakespearean actor and a confident filmmaker. *Hamlet* was his third film interpretation of a Shakespeare play (following on from *Henry V* (1989) and 1993's delightful *Much Ado About Nothing*). The previous year he'd even made a film about a bunch of actors performing the play in a village — *A Midwinter's Tale* (1995) — so you could say he was poised to make his version.

The fact that he performed the entire soliloquy in front of a full-length mirror — slowly walking towards his own reflection — speaks of his confidence in himself as both Actor and Filmmaker. No doubt, several takes of the shot, following the Actor from a full-length reflection in the mirror into a medium close-up, were made — for 'safety' and for the right performance. Nevertheless, the intent was to perform the famous lines in a SINGLE shot. That's *'tour-de-force'* stuff right there.

Before Branagh begins to speak, we are shown that the mirror he faces is of the 'two-way' variety and he is being observed by 'Claudius' (Derek Jacobi) and 'Polonius' (Richard Briers). This gives Branagh the opportunity for a brief CUTAWAY to 'Claudius' 'behind the mirror'. Although, during the soliloquy itself, only these two shots appear in the film, I suspect there were reverse shots made 'through the mirror' of Branagh — shots that would be the POV (point of view) of 'Claudius' and 'Polonius'. It seems unlikely to me that you wouldn't 'cover' the entire soliloquy from the REVERSE angle — so that there would always be some way out of the dilemma if the OTS (over the shoulder) TRUCKING from a FULL to MEDIUM CLOSE-UP shot used in the film hadn't quite worked.

We shall learn more about these various Shots as we continue. But first, let's jump to the Cutaway — The Ultimate Safety Shot. You may never need your Cutaway, and certainly you might not intend to have a Cutaway as part of one of your scenes. But… if all else fails, if there is absolutely nothing that can be done and a reshoot is out of the question… go to the inanimate object. It might look a bit 'soft-core porno' but it's better than cutting in a black leader slug with a Super that says; *"Sorry, folks, messed up bad. Normal footage will be restored when the camera gets back in focus".*

I worked with a Director many times who would never leave a scene, a set, nor a location without taking 15 minutes to shoot as many Cutaways as he could — the clock, the pen lying on the desk, the view into the garden, the book on the side-table. I don't think he ever used them. But he had them.

With Cutaways discussed and filed away in the recesses of your mind, and this brief explanation of 'Coverage' given — allow me to develop an argument for creating a Shot List. A strategy laid out to take you successfully through your shoot. Although plenty of filmmakers find making a Shot List to be tiresome, it needn't be overly hard work. A Shot List contains as much or as little information as you need. But like anything else, the more effort you put into it — the better your result. To be effective you will need to consider three things about the Shot you intend to make — these being the basic elements of your List, and the building blocks of your style.

The Frame. The Motion. The Means.

CHAPTER TWO

Elements of Style

There are those who don't make Shot Lists, but who 'Storyboard' or 'Pre-Viz' instead. Some make thumbnail sketches in the margins of their scripts, or jot down quick notes discernable only to them. There are directors who rehearse, or workshop, scenes with the cast and 'see' the intended shots. Others wait until they have their cast 'on-set' and then block the performance — waiting until that final moment (with the Cinematographer beside them) to decide on how to shoot the scene. All well and good, but no matter what approach is taken, it's important to be able to communicate.

We have to have a way to describe what is 'in the frame', with a degree of exactness that is understandable and immediate. If you say to your Cinematographer that the next shot should be a MEDIUM CLOSE-UP, you will be understood. Of course, there is no single lens, or camera position, that gives you a MEDIUM CLOSE-UP, far less the shot that has been lurking in your imagination. The Cinematographer doesn't reach into a Pelican case and bring out the MEDIUM CLOSE-UP lens. But, in requesting a MEDIUM CLOSE-UP, everyone involved will be on roughly the same page. We're professionals, after all. We know what a MEDIUM CLOSE-UP is supposed to look like. If someone backstage in the Make-Up Dept asks a passing 2nd A.D. 'What's the next Set-up?', and the reply is 'MEDIUM CLOSE-UP', then that information will be understood and perhaps acted upon. But 'how' that MEDIUM CLOSE-UP will be framed is something that only occurs in the moment, on the set — when the Director matches their 'idea' of the shot to the reality in front of the lens. We might say ME-DIUM CLOSE-UP, but to write it down constantly is tedious — even if it's only to label a frame in a Storyboard or pencil an instruction to yourself in the script margins. Thankfully, shot descriptions can be expressed in shorthand ways. Using a variety of still images from *The Missing Link*, a 'micro-budget' film I directed some years ago, here's a lexicon of those abbreviations and a brief description of what they mean;

EST — Establishing

We all know this one. The often-tedious shot that tells the audience where the action is to be played out or implies where the characters are. (Sometimes it is a shot used to tell the audience where 'they' are — but don't worry, only 'experimental' and 'art-house' genres tend to play those games). Actually, this is a shot you should pay attention to. If it hasn't been carefully considered it can very quickly devalue your production. You should be seeking to enhance the tone of your film, to suggest mood and atmosphere, to invest the simple idea of location with some depth. Even a shot that is of 'nothing at all' — a field of grass, for example — can be heavy with 'presence', with season, with the passage of time, with 'expectation'. There's a great deal more that can be 'established' in an Establishing Shot than a mere physical location.

Director of Photography
DAVID LASSITER

The still image on the previous page shows an establishing shot which is a little different from the usual cityscape or building exterior. I should mention that although the excellent David Lassiter was, as the credit shows, Cinematographer on *The Missing Link*, this shot was made by 2nd Unit Director of Photography, Matt Irwin. Please note that the shot is attempting to establish; (i) a pristine wilderness, (ii) the isolation and vulnerability of the human figure and (iii) a vast and inhospitable landscape. It's also doing something subliminally — or that is the intention — (iv) to make the audience think that they are about to watch a movie with a significant budget shot in a 'cinematic' style. In other words, making the audience unaware of the film's 'micro-budget'.

MAS — Master

A shot, wide enough to take in all the relevant information present in the scene, and which 'covers' all the action and dialogue. Sometimes, a Master will be broken up with one shot for the start of the scene (the first 90 seconds perhaps) and another for the end. The example below is a Master intercut into a scene 3 times, for a total of 17 seconds.

Alternatively, a scene can be broken into a series of Master Shots, each 'covering' a separate part of the action/dialogue — usually with a change of angle.

WS — Wide

When not used in the sense of a 'Master', a 'Wide' shot is harder to define. It's a shot that gives a feeling of horizontal space, whether that's in a landscape or a closet.

LS — Long

What's the difference between a Wide and a Long Shot? The difference is most noticeable in confined environments. Disregarding, for the present, the effect of various lenses, if we assume that we have a 'standard human' view of a subject, then a Long Shot is like standing at the back of a theater watching actors on stage.

A Wide Shot, on the other hand, is similar to sitting in the front row of the theater, able to see the entire stage. If we think of a director in love with the LS, we might consider David Lean. Like the work of John Ford, many of Lean's most famous shots are WIDE, but the most memorable — Omar Sharif riding out of the desert towards camera in *Lawrence of Arabia* (1965) — is LONG. In fact, it's So Incredibly Long... we should probably call it...

ELS — Extreme Long Shot

... one of these. Here's a shot from *The Missing Link* which I consider an ELS. I marched the camera crew a quarter-mile away from the 'action' (cavemen running from a CGI saber-tooth tiger). The shot is indeed wide, but it's the length that interested me and that's why I notated it as ELS in my Shot List.

And because I love the ELS so much, here's another...

You can barely see the tiny figure of the main character (played by K.C. Morgan as 'Patrick') walking (L-R) along the beach, but… if you follow the shot above with the shot below…

… you've brought the audience from an overview of the 'Special World' of the story — right into the action.

Before we leave the LS — different lenses will, of course, give you different effects, but a shot can still be a Long Shot whether the lens is 200mm or 40mm, depending on the distance between subject and camera. For example, here's the LS of the cavemen running towards camera, shot with a 'long' lens (probably 105mm or greater), from a considerable distance.

The 'long' lens was chosen to make the actors seem more bunched up… and to bring them 'closer' to camera while throwing the background out of focus.

FS — Full Shot

In the above shot, K.C. Morgan is moving from a FS to a MEDIUM shot to pick up the object in right foreground. A Full Shot is a 'full figure' of the subject, but the choice of lens will determine how 'wide' shot becomes. If I'd requested a change to a 'longer' lens for this shot (say, from 24mm to 40mm) and placed the camera further back, K.C. Morgan would have remained 'full figure' (and thus, an FS) but the view would have been 'narrower' — losing much of the rockface to the right of the foreground object and the beach on the left.

Sometimes you might want to make a note in your Shot List regarding the lens you intend to discuss with your Cinematographer — because your choice of lens has a profound effect on how an audience both 'sees' and 'feels' the image. For now, I'll keep that information to a minimum, and save a more detailed discussion regarding how directors use lenses for another fine volume in *The Filmmaker's Art* series.

MS — Medium

More than just about every other Shot description, 'Medium' is a vague term, a shot that we tend to know only when we see it.

For example, the 3-Shot below could be described as MS… and equally well be described as 'MEDIUM-WIDE'…

How would you notate the shot? MS/WS seems too vague. Can you hear the Cinematographer ask; *'Well, which is it?'* In this case, I would have suggested that the MS framing keep the interest on the center figure (Michael King as 'Grog') yet be 'wide' enough to keep Dan Sheldon (as 'Stein') and Sean Ridgway (as 'Kooter') in frame.

The above shot of Ian Jerrell (as 'Bruno') is MS too, despite being 'closer' than the previous frame. The point is this; you notate a Shot List to formulate a plan. Using lens choice and camera placement, you finalize that plan when the actors are on-set. You know going in that you want a Medium shot, but until you see the frame in the camera you don't have to make a final decision as to how 'tight' or 'loose' that MS might be.

MCU — Medium Close-Up

Again, the MCU can cover a lot of ground because it's not completely specific. It's a shot that gets used very frequently because it's so flexible. It brings the audience into the subject without being overwhelming...

Here's a 'loose' MCU of Laura Shields (as 'Ana'), that allows us to read her expression and thought, without taking us too close into the character's reaction or emotion.

The MCU shot is used in this frame in a 'wider' sense, not only to easily see K.C. Morgan's expression/reaction but also get a clear understanding of the environment/situation.

A final MCU example shows a frame that combines 'width' and yet allows us a 'close-up' of three characters — Ian Jerrell (as 'Bruno'), Dan Sheldon (as 'Stein') and Sean Ridgway (as 'Kooter').

CU — Close-Up

A classic CU. Here, Mark Mainardi (as 'Nug') is framed so that the audience is brought in close to the character — a shot that is used sparingly in 'theatrical' films but is used more frequently in 'televisual' projects where a smaller screen requires closer framing to capture details of human expression that can get 'lost'. Notice that the framing 'cuts off' the actor from mid-brow upwards so as gets a close shot without unbalancing important areas of the face. You might also want to note that the

mouth is in the lower third of third of frame and the eyes in the upper third — a compositional tool to achieve balance.
ECU — Extreme Close-Up

The obvious difference when distinguishing between a CU and an ECU of an actor's face is that the ECU frames the 'interior' of the face. Above, the shot of Michael King (as 'Grog) has an intensity that a CU wouldn't achieve. In truth, this is a 'loose' ECU — the shot is more familiar when the framing is tighter. This one of Ian Jerrell (as 'Bruno) shows that better — and, of course, you can go all the way into an eyeball if that works.

ECUs are common for important details of inanimate objects, but the trick is to make the ECU interesting and not banal, without being weird. The more inanimate the object — the harder, somehow, it is to film. So, it's a shot that can become time-consuming — as you will discover if you find yourself in-carcerated in the joyless prison that is television commercials production.

2SH — 2 Shot

K.C. Morgan (as 'Patrick') and Percy Rusty (as 'Sven') demon-strate the 2-Shot.

Mark Mainardi (as 'Nug') and Michael King (as 'Grog') share a 2-Shot, from a side angle. The shot is 'raked' — meaning that the actors are in a line but positioned so each is seen. 2-Shots tend to be 'medium' or 'medium-close'. When the D.P. asks if the next shot is to be a 2-Shot, it's really 'on-set' shorthand to describe two actors in the frame. It's not strictly a 'shot size' — but the common understanding is that it will be MS or MCU.

S/C — Clean Single

Again, you'll often be asked if you want to shoot a 'Single' and if that 'Single' should be 'Clean' or 'Dirty'. This S/C of Laura Shields ('Ana') is a MS. You'll sometimes hear this framing described as 'Head and Shoulders'. Go ahead and put H&S into your Shot List if that makes you comfortable. In this case, because the scene is about a woman trying to make a romantic connection with a man she is attracted to, I used the S/C because I wanted Laura to literally be a 'single woman'. To be alone in the frame. That was the important part of the notation. I knew I could frame her from 'Medium-Wide' to 'Medium-Close' and get what was required — but I waited until I was on-set before I made a final decision on shot 'size'.

S/D — Dirty Single

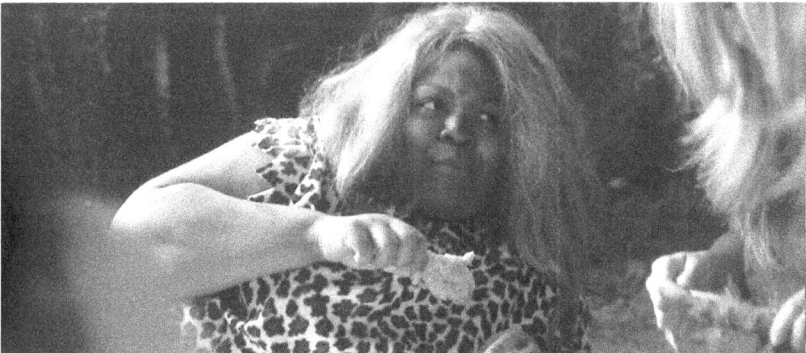

The 'Dirty Single' shot is all about one performer, but some part of another actor, (their shoulder/back of head, jaw etc.,) is also in shot, generally out of focus and 'dirtying' the frame. In the frame previously, the fabulous Chenese Lewis (as 'Femalé') is lying on her side, with two other actors kneeling on each side of her. Notice how placing the other actors partially in shot creates a 'frame within a frame', drawing our attention inwards.

In the S/D below, Alan English (as 'Ty') looks up at Chenese Lewis whose body and right forearm are fully in left frame.

Notice again how a 'Dirty Single' throws the audience's entire attention onto the subject. Our brains know that the out-of-focus portion of the shot is not important other than for spatial information, so we zero in on the area of the screen that the director wants us to look at. And, of course, you don't need an actor to 'dirty' the frame. Inanimate objects work just as well.

REV – A Reverse switches the audience's point of view 180° from the previous shot. When shooting dialogue scenes involving two (or more) actors, the Reverse will generally be a close mirror image of the first shot in terms of the angle, the lens size and the framing. So here we go from Alan to…

… Chenese. In this case, the Reverse is not only 'Clean', it is also a different focal length (size) than the shot that preceded it — and is clearly not the desired 'mirror image'. *Mea culpa*. This Reverse would have been technically better if it had 'matched' the previous shot and been 'Dirty' too, with Alan's left shoulder in bottom right of frame. But hey, in 'micro-budget' world, the pace of shooting is faster than a speeding bullet. Tidy, techni-cally-correct approaches get forgotten or discarded, forcing choices that may not be "traditional" or completely "correct".

OTS – Over-The-Shoulder

The OTS is a specific kind of REVERSE used in a dialogue scene between two or more actors. It's not quite the same as a 'Dirty Single', because it usually involves seeing the jaw move-ment of the actor with their back/shoulder to camera – which means dialogue must be delivered correctly. Yes, audiences do notice if a jaw is moving in such a way that it doesn't match the words they're hearing on the soundtrack.

The following shot is not, strictly speaking, a 'Dirty Single' on K.C. Morgan's 'Patrick', but nor is it a conventional OTS either.

Why? Mostly because Laura Shields (as 'Ana') is completely in the frame, albeit with her back to camera. If there had been an out-of-focus 'portion' of her in frame, then this shot would have been a true 'Dirty Single'. But it's not — and that was deliberate. We're all capable of reading human reaction even when someone has their back to us. By including more of 'Ana' in the frame, the balance of audience interest and attention is split between the two characters. The shot is weighted towards 'Patrick'... but we can sense how 'Ana' is reacting.

Although the Reverse in the above frame does allow us to 'read' K.C. Morgan's jawline, once again this is not a conventional OTS. *'Why isn't the shot positioned more definitively over-the-shoulder?'* you ask, with perfect logic. I can't remember precisely why, but probably because I wanted the audience to get a clearer sense of male discomfort, and a better idea of the space between 'Ana' and 'Patrick'. It's essentially a 2-SHOT, this time with the interest pushed towards 'Ana'.

Are you getting the idea that, sometimes, there is no hard distinction between various shots? Good, because it's true. Shot descriptions, and the Shot List itself, are merely devices to help you move from Shot to Shot. Merely a starting point for your Set-Up that can be further adjusted and refined.

Let's look at a true OTS...

In this scene, Hilary Novelle Hahn (as 'Fugly') tears into Michael King (as 'Grog') while Leanne Slaby (as 'Muff') and Laura Shields (as 'Ana') look on. Michael can deliver lines accurately, take after take, so he can be shot OTS with confidence.

- *Uh, what?*

Just something to reiterate. From this OTS angle, as Michael responds to Hilary, we can see his jaw moving. Which means he has to say the right words. If he mangles the response lines to Hilary, we could 'fix it in post' and put the right lines in from another take — but they are unlikely to be in sync. That 'fix it in post' will quickly become a series of 'fix solutions' that might end up in an expensive ADR session. We can't afford that.

Hilary can deliver lines perfectly every time too, so why is the above Reverse not a true OTS? Well, her hair covered her jawline anyway, and I wanted to back away a little so as to get a sense of Leanne on the far left of frame. Also, I didn't ask D.P. David Lassiter to lower the camera to get Hilary's shoulder in frame as that would have given too 'heavy' and 'dominant' an angle on Michael. He would have towered over Hilary. I wanted a 'straight-on' confrontation because, in this scene, the character's patriarchy is being questioned. So, not a true OTS — but a decently conceived REVERSE.

Here's a couple of 'true' OTS shots. The characters (Dan Sheldon (as 'Stein'), Michael King (as 'Grog') are arguing.

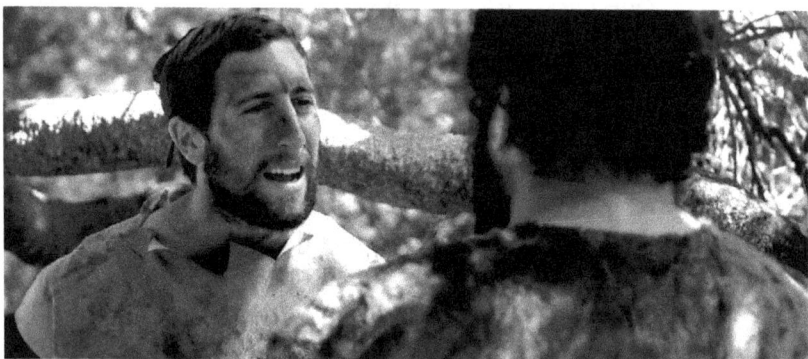

'Grog' is being challenged by 'Stein' for the leadership of the tribe — so there's a subtle difference in height and angle between the two frames.

These subtle differences in lens height, and the balance you place between characters, are important considerations — which sometimes warrant a note to yourself in your Shot List.

POV — Point-Of-View of a character.

First, establish who is doing the 'looking'…

… and then show what is being 'looked at'…

(For the classic example of an over-the-top use, watch *The Lady In The Lake* (1947) — an entire film shot in the POV of the 'Philip Marlowe' character, directed by Robert Montgomery).

C/WAY — I made this last one up. I've never seen an abbreviation for a Cutaway, just as I've never seen a Shot List indicate that a particular shot would be used as a 'Cutaway'. Instead you'll get something like... ECU — Ming Vase on Table.

CHAPTER THREE

Ways and Means

One of the primary elements of the 'style' you develop as a filmmaker is how you frame your shots, a subject we shall deal with extensively in Vol. 4 of the series — *Eye of a Poet*. But the building blocks of your style are in the shots that you use. We've looked at the Basic Sixteen — EST, MAS, WS, LS, ELS, FS, MS, MCU, CU, ECU, 2SH, S/C, S/D, REV, OTS, POV.

You could stop right there, make a List using a variety of those shots, and get through production with no problem. But if we consider that one of the purposes of creating a Shot List is to help you think through how you will shoot the scenes that you are preparing, then we should continue and be completist. This next batch covers camera placement or positioning.

- AERIAL — Aerial Shot, (nowadays mostly from a Drone).
- TOP — Top Shot (aka Bird's Eye View or Overhead)
- HI-ANG — High Angle
- LO-ANG — Low Angle
- EYE — Eye Level
- DUTCH/CANT or ROLL — a Shot where the axis/angle is canted to some degree, including a 360° rotation.

That's simple enough — your notations MS/LO-ANG and CU/DUTCH are now easy and familiar… but wait, there's more.

If you consider that a Shot List is a reminder to yourself of *what* you're going to shoot, it is also a reminder of *how* you are going to shoot. Most directors incorporate camera movement into their Shot Lists. Abbreviations get a little silly at this point, and so you'll mostly find these terms;

FIXED — A set, static Frame — that might move to hold the subject in the shot if there is movement within the frame.

LOCKED — A fixed Frame that on no account is moved, usually because something is going to be introduced into the Frame that requires a static composition — most often a post-production VFX.

PAN — A horizontal movement from Frame A to Frame B. A movement that could either be made hand-held or supported in a variety of ways, the most common being a tripod with a fluid-head. In the Shot List you would normally indicate the Left/Right motion as in; PAN/MS L to R —JACK to JOHN.

WHIP — A fast, sometimes 'blurry', Pan, most commonly accomplished with a hand-held camera. WHIP/MS R to L

TILT — A vertical movement from Frame A to Frame B.

TRACK — Tracking at a 90° angle to the subject. Moving Left to Right or vice-versa, sometimes referred to as a Crab Shot — incorrectly in my opinion. Traditionally, a Tracking Shot was made on a Dolly moving along tracks, but it can be made with stabilizer equipment and drones or, in its simplest form, Hand-Held. TRACK/FS with JACK

A Tracking Shot can also be made on a tripod fixed to one spot. *'What's that?'* you cry, in astonished disbelief. *'How?'*

Patience, dear reader — that's a teaser for a future discussion on the 'Kurosawa Dolly' which we will find in the 'motion' section of *The Filmmaker's Art Vol. 4. Eye of A Poet.*

CRAB — A type of Tracking Shot commonly using a three-wheeled 'Crab Dolly' or 'Pedestal'. The camera has a 45° angle to the subject as it moves, giving a diagonal, rather than straight line 180° 'feel' to the movement. You're going to need to watch your focus. A 'Crab Dolly' is an interesting beast and will give you access to all kinds of neat angularities in relation to your subject. Be aware that operating a 'Crab Dolly' is a skill and not as easy as it looks.

TRUCK — Often referred to as Tracking — which is fine, but incorrect. To 'Truck' the camera is to move the camera in a straight line in a forward motion. For example, a shot that moves towards an object or subject. The Subject might be an actor walking towards a camera that is 'trucking' towards the actor, or it could be a camera following an actor who is walking in front of the lens. Either way, it's 'trucking' because the forward motion is in a straight line relative to the object or subject. Sometimes notated as TRUCK IN.

REV TRUCK — Keep on 'trucking', but this time the camera motion is backwards, or reversed from a forward motion 'Truck In'. Often used with an actor walking towards camera, with camera and actor moving at the same speed, thus keeping the same distance throughout. Alternatively, the subject (actor) or object (dead body) could be static and the camera 'reverse trucks' away. You could also get a very nice effect by having an actor walk away while the camera 'reverse trucks' in the opposite direction. Sometimes notated as TRUCK OUT.

To be fair, both TRUCK and REV TRUCK are falling into disuse, largely because the terms have been confused for too long with TRACKING. A good alternative is to use PUSH and PULL instead, although an 'old school' guy like me doesn't necessarily think of PUSH and PULL as having the specific quality of movement that TRUCK or REV TRUCK describes.

Lastly, we have some tags and descriptions that indicate the means by which you will create the shot. Most are very obvious and, as we shall see, are used to more fully de-scribe how the shot will be set up.

STICKS — Using some form of Tripod. In my Shot Lists I usu-ally get more detailed and use terms like BABY LEGS or per-haps HIHAT to indicate equipment that will give me a ground level, or very LO-ANGLE shot — and TALL STICKS to specify that the tripod should be extended above shoulder height.

P/F — PULL FOCUS. One of the most powerful tools in a filmmaker's repertoire is the 'focus pull'. It's not something to be over-used, but it is an entirely visual way to 'sell' an idea or feeling. In the Frames below, the first shot has Leanne Slaby (as 'Muff') in sharp focus, while Laura Shields (as 'Ana') is soft.

In the storyline, 'Ana' has told a lie and it bothers her. 'Muff' has just realized that something is not right. She stays in focus

long enough for the audience to understand that… and then the 1st Assistant Camera Person (a.k.a. the Focus Puller) shifts that sharp focus to 'Ana' so that the audience sees her conflicted expression.

H/H — HAND-HELD. Not just a means to get a shot, sometimes it's a whole style. Properly operated, going Hand-Held often contributes more to the dynamic and emotional nature of the footage than to its movement. I might indulge in a rant here because constant H/H is the most over-used, slapped-together, boring, irritating and unimaginative shooting-style ever presented to a long-suffering public. But let's move on.

STEADI — Used exclusively in the days when Steadicam™ was the principal camera stabilizer, and still used today by people like me although we know that there are multiple systems out there. I suppose I could use GIMB for a gimbal-based system, but as most Hand-Held shots are now gimbal-assisted I don't want to confuse you. Or me. Mostly me.

CRANE —Crane Shot. Note that I'm *not* specifying what type of Crane, merely indicating a crane is to be used. I usually will indicate a start and end position in the List. WS/CRANE/HI-ANG on rooftop, DESCEND to doorway.

BOOM — another way to describe a CRANE shot, but BOOM implies a vertical movement from low to high, or vice-versa. Bear in mind that because a CRANE can be used on a horizontal axis as well as vertical, and can also PUSH and PULL, using BOOM, in my opinion, denotes a movement that doesn't have a horizontal element.

SLIDER — Micro-Budget Producers, Directors and Cinematographers get very excited about the possibilities opened up with the use of a Slider. It's an interesting tool (if it can be kept stable) and allows filmmakers, on tight budgets in tight spaces, to get some movement that might not otherwise be available to them. Again, I will indicate how the equipment will be used — as in; MCU/ SLIDER/TRACK L-R

DRONE — I might use term this rather than AERIAL. We live in a blessed world, able to use drones for huge, bird's eye vistas for a fraction of the cost of a helicopter. Drones are also capable of making Tracking and Trucking shots. Thus, I might indicate; DRONE/TRUCK OUT w/subject thru' doorway to EXT and RISE to ELS/HI-ANG, subject in center-frame.

LO-RIDER — I use this one when I want to make shots using a Process Trailer or Insert Car to film actors driving vehicles. Sometimes I don't know what kind of equipment I'm ultimately going to use to make a shot. My initial request might get turned down by a producer due to equipment cost or availability.

Here's a couple of shots that appear on those 'How To' informational materials offered for free on the internet in exchange for your email. I have never seen these on any Shot List.

Ever.

CHOKER — Apparently, a 'Choker' is the type of CLOSE-UP that frames an actor's face from mid-brow to mid-chin. Easier just to remember ECU.

ITALIAN — Oh, dear. This really does appear on some 'Info' lists. It's another name for an ECU — the name presumably deriving from 'Spaghetti Westerns' and the shots Sergio Leone made for the final shoot-out in *The Good, The Bad and The Ugly* (1966) of squinting eyes, and nervously-licked lips.

The next two are rapidly going into disuse — but there's a chance you'll hear them, particularly this one...

COWBOY — This is a shot derived from the Westerns that used to be so much a part of Hollywood filmmaking. You might still hear some Cinematographers use the term, and it's also called an 'AMERICAN' on occasion. (Not to be confused with an 'American Cut' which is a sequence of 3 or 4 shots taken with increasingly 'longer' lenses, framed on a precise linear trajectory, and edited in rapid succession.... and if that sounds complicated, I'm attempting to describe those shock 'jump' cuts from wide into close-up that we've all seen a million times). The COWBOY or AMERICAN is a 'loose' MEDIUM shot, whereby the subject is framed from the knees upwards presumably so that we can see the hero's six guns in their holsters. Not to be confused with COWGIRL and its companion REVERSE COWGIRL, which are terms used in the production of filmed adult entertainment wherein a performer sits astride another performer in either a traditional or 'reverse' manner. Don't ask me how I know this.

WARNER CUT/FRAMING — Sometimes, if the crew is composed of very old people, you'll hear the director — okay, you'll hear me — say to the Cinematographer; 'Give me a Close-Up with a Warner Framing'. This is a close-up framing on an actor's face that cuts off the top of the head from mid-brow — but includes the chin, so it's not the aforesaid 'Choker'. I don't know the provenance of this expression, but presumably it derives from some long-forgotten house style originating in that lovely studio at the intersection of Barham and Hollywood Way.

In conclusion. This is not a "complete" list of possible shots and their descriptions/abbreviations, but they are the most common and you'll become more familiar as we go on.

I'm going to stay 'old school' with my use of these abbreviations and the formulation of a Shot List. It's my preferred method — but it doesn't have to be yours. If you ultimately reject Shot Listing in this way, and find it is not something you choose to do then, at the very least, find an approach that is both efficient and understandable to you. Nobody cares if your Shot List is a mess of arcane symbols, dotted lines, weird directional arrows and thumbnail drawings. Well, they might —

but as long as *you* know what it all means, you've met the principal requirement. *How* you do it doesn't matter. *Why* you do it does.

There are those who will continue to resist the very idea of a Shot List, believing that they can keep it all in their head, or be able to react to the moment. But feature films are long, drawn-out affairs, with a multitude of distractions and anxieties. The job of a film director is rather like being the conductor of a large, unruly orchestra. Until you are fully experienced and deeply familiar with what you are doing, you're going to need to glance at the music sheets once in a while. Your Shot List is your personal road map through the movie you are making. Without it — everyone may become lost. Especially you.

Who gets your List? That's for you to decide. Today's Shot List apps (such as StudioBinder.com) not only give you fast, flexible and efficient ways of building your List, but allow you to share it with as many collaborators as you wish. I've always treated a Shot List as a document that, if not exactly 'Top Secret', is distributed on a 'Need-To-Know' basis to a select few. I always give a copy to the 1st Assistant Director because she needs to be several steps ahead of me in the game — so that actors and elements arrive in the right place at the right time. Directors of Photography ask for one — but I've noticed it usually gets folded up and stuffed in a back pocket and seldom consulted. Unit Production Managers are flattered when you give them a Shot List, but it's not particularly useful to them and they lose it amongst the piles of other paperwork they have. Actors do not need one. Some will come and look over your shoulder when you're consulting yours and I, for one, tolerate this, but it's easier, more personal and much more effective to give actors information orally rather than hand them the whole plan. For some directors, doling out bite-sized pieces of information 'as-and-when-required' is the best method of dealing with both cast and crew.

I've heard the Coen Brothers have an interesting technique which goes counter to what I've just said. Every day they hand out 'Sides' to the actors (the script pages of the scene(s) to be shot that day). Along with the 'Sides' come small storyboard diagrams so that each actor knows how the scene is going to be 'covered' and shot. That's a very intense and intricately-planned way of working – but it probably helps reduce the amount of communication required and speeds up the day. It also allows the actors to get an idea of how they will be physically moved through the space, and how intimate — or not — the shots are going to be.

Do actors need to know what 'size' of Shot you are about to shoot? Some of them do, because they are experienced enough to adjust their performance depending on how 'big' they will appear in the frame. There are some actors who will even ask you, or the Cinematographer, what lens is on the camera — so that they can make a performance adjustment — just as there are actors who understand what the lighting is going to do to their appearance and what positioning gives them the best and most flattering light.

If you don't have a Shot List you will very quickly lose pace and flow not only in the physical work, but also in the movie itself. You will also be unsure as to the Coverage you are getting and will not be able to take advantage of the 'moments' that occur during filming which allow you to add a new idea or explore a different approach. If you have a Shot List, you can step onto a movie set anywhere in the world — and direct. Crews follow Captains. On a film set, the Captain is the person who has formulated, and who understands, the Shot List. So, please. No more discussion on whether we should have a Shot List or not.

But how do we *build* a Shot List?

CHAPTER FOUR

The Build

When people talk about the Grammar or Vocabulary of Film it's just a fancy way of discussing the Framing, Composition and Editing of Shots that we all know from the films and television we have seen. We don't have to invent it. We have to keep it fresh. What you are seeking to achieve as a director is to film a scene with economy, style, precision and 'safety', using all the technical means at your disposal.

Let's say you have a short scene written like this...

```
16. EXT. ABANDONED FACTORY. DAWN.

Jack's BMW appears, tires squealing, and skids
to a stop. JACK leaps out, gun in his hand,
runs through a gap in a sagging perimeter fence
and kicks open the door into the building.
```

That's a short scene. As detailed in *Selecting For Success*, during the Pre-Production phase the U.P.M and/or 1st A.D. will have broken the screenplay down and decided that Sc. 16 equals 1/8th of a script page. The Scene would have gone into the Breakdown alongside other scenes to be shot at the 'Abandoned Factory' location and will have become part of your scheduled workday.

Your Art Department, Location Manager, Stunt Coordinator, Camera, Sound, Make-up & Hair and Costume Departments will have taken your earlier pre-production briefings, 'feelings', comments, notes — along with your responses to their questions — and will have everything you need ready on the set/location to shoot Sc. 16 before DAWN breaks on the Scheduled Day. This will include the sagging perimeter FENCE, the BMW, the actor playing JACK, the correct COSTUME Jack will be wearing (bearing in mind continuity from previous scenes), the GUN -- and the PRECISION DRIVER if it's decided that the actor playing JACK can't, or shouldn't, drive the car in the aggressive way the script calls for.

Those are the obvious things. What is less obvious is how you are going to shoot the scene, with the implication of what equipment you will need. When you 'walked' the location in a Pre-Production 'Tech Scout' several weeks previously, your Cinematographer would have asked what you had in mind.

If you'd read *Selecting For Success*, I'd like to think you had a response. But, guess what? Back on that 'tech recce', you didn't *need* to have an answer. In Pre-Production, when a director can't, or won't, give an answer to a question then everyone scurries around and gets prepared for all eventualities, so that their collective butts are completely covered. If this causes possible additional charges for equipment rentals or additional personnel, then the department with the problem runs and tells the Line Producer, who tells the Producer, who comes to you and asks what you're planning. You can still shrug and say you don't know, and you might get a cold stare — or you might get treated like a genius in embryo. More directors than you can shake a stick at have sequences or scenes where they don't have a clue as to how to proceed and are simply going to show up on the day and hope for the best.

There's a classic tale about Roman Polanski on *Repulsion* (1970) shooting a CLOSE-UP of a hand picking up scissors — take after take after take — and driving his producer nuts. Why was Polanski wasting so much time on a simple shot of relatively minor importance? Because he was giving himself time to figure out what to do in the scene he had to shoot *next*!

A more specific 'pre-production' example is of Kubrick sending out a scout to find a red-painted door for a brief moment in *Eyes Wide Shut* (1999). The poor guy photographed every red door in London. Took him weeks. Kubrick hated them all. So, at the last minute, he had his Art Dept. build a set to his precise specification.

What is film directing anyway? It's a process of unique selection. The director's selection. The director's individual way of telling a story. Those initial selections made in Pre-Production are further refined in the Shot List.

So, let us imagine that you didn't have a complete idea, when you 'scouted' the location, as to how you would shoot Sc. 16 and all the other scenes that will be filmed at the 'Abandoned Factory'. During your 'scout', all you knew was that the location 'worked' for the story. Now, here you are in your hotel room, in the last week of Pre-Production. You've read Sc. 16 and absorbed its details. You're going to turn up in the dark one morning soon and forty people will want to know what they have to do before the sun rises. The shots that you choose to make, and later assemble, are yours alone. Give Sc. 16 to ten different directors and each one of them will tell the story of the car arriving and the man with the gun jumping out and running into the building in a *different* way. Each director will make his or her own unique selections of how to present Sc. 16 to an audience. Some will focus on how to make the scene visually arresting. Some will seek to create a mood that may not be in the written words — but fits into their 'vision' of the film. Some may think Sc. 16 is unimportant and needs to be ignored. Some are only thinking about how to shoot it quickly and move on.

Sc. 16 is, for now, part of your story. How important a part you have to decide from your reading of the entire script. How you bring that decision into the editing room for final consideration is dependent on the most important scrap of paper you will have in your hand all day. No, not the script — the Shot List. Find a pencil. Grab a legal pad. Read Sc. 16 again.

```
16. EXT. ABANDONED FACTORY. DAWN.

Jack's BMW appears, tires squealing, and skids
to a stop. JACK leaps out, gun in his hand,
runs through a gap in a sagging perimeter fence
and kicks open the door into the building.
```

A Scene Heading and four Action lines. A total page count of 1/8th of a page. One shot or six? You decide. Here's what will make your mind up. Time. How much time do you have to shoot? If you start shooting at 6 a.m. and the schedule says that you *also* have to shoot Scs. 89 & 91 at this location and then make a 10-minute company move to be at the next location for breakfast at 8.30 a.m., then you can't get crazy. You have a tad under 2.5 hours to shoot three scenes.

Think about this '1/8th of a page' business. We went through it in detail in *Selecting For Success*. But here's the take-away for those who might not have read that fine book and a recap for those who did and who enjoy the *frisson d'horreur* that comes from the knowledge that the moment you set foot on a film set — Time, as the song says, is running out.

The majority of 'low-budget independent' features are shot on 18-day or 24-day schedules. Some are much less. 10 or 12 days are the 'norm' for many of the films in the 'creature-feature' or 'horror' genres. With minimal shooting schedules, the daily shoot/page ratio jumps to disturbing size. Let's do the math. An 85-page screenplay on a 10-day shooting schedule?

8 and 4/8ths per day. That's challenging. A 108 page 'low-budget indie' on an 18-day schedule? 6 pages a day. Not so bad, but still tough if you care about the details. When you know your schedule and your daily page rate, then you can quickly work out how fast you have to shoot. Let's imagine that you've been given 20 days at 10 hours per day, to shoot a 100-page screenplay. 100/20 = 5 pages/day. Our shoot day is 10 hours? Thus, we have to shoot a page-worth (8/8ths) of our screenplay every 2 hours. Divide 120 minutes by 8 and we find that we need to shoot $1/8^{th}$ every 15 minutes. Bear that last result in mind, if you will.

Once again, you read Sc. 16.

```
16. EXT. ABANDONED FACTORY. DAWN.

Jack's BMW appears, tires squealing, and skids
to a stop. JACK leaps out, gun in his hand,
runs through a gap in a sagging perimeter fence
and kicks open the door into the building.
```

One-eighth of a page. And you have 15 minutes to shoot it. Ah, Time. My Enemy. I can't stop you screaming out. You will indeed suck the life out of me.

Your close friends and supportive allies — U.P.M and/or 1st A.D.— have gone over the script in detail. They've noted Sc. 16 is 1/8th, and seen it involves a car – so in their experience they figure you'll shoot out the scene in 30 minutes. They know that is double the limit allotted 'per schedule', but the way they see it you can go "over" on your time budget on certain scenes because you'll "catch up" on easier scenes later on — like extended interior dialogue scenes where a couple of characters sit on a couch and talk for five minutes. They're figuring that over the long haul there will be days when you'll be able to knock off five pages or so in well under the allotted time and the schedule will balance out. They take a look at Scenes 89 and 91, and notice that these scenes are also short. They decide that Sc. 89 is also $1/8^{th}$, and Sc. 91 is 2/8ths. For the location we're calling 'Abandoned Factory, the three scenes together total 4/8ths of a page. They multiple 15 minutes by 4 and reckon that 60 minutes is all the time required to keep *on schedule* but, following their thinking on Sc. 16, they are prepared to give you 'double' time to complete the three scenes. 2 hours in total.

Given the 6 a.m. call-time, a minor company move and 8.30 breakfast — that should work out just fine. Satisfied that another scheduling problem has been successfully dealt with, your team moves onto other matters and Scs. 16, 89 & 91 are locked into the production schedule.

Yes, it's easy to calculate Time when you're sitting in a production office. We've done the convoluted math – and it all seems perfectly reasonable. Now that we know how much Time is allocated to the scene, our next question is;

- *What needs to be accomplished in the time frame?*

Actually, this is not your next question — but let's just follow it for now until we reach the dead-end it leads to. You are now aware that you have been given 30 minutes to shoot Sc.16. What happens in the scene? A car drives up to an abandoned building; a character gets out and goes inside. You've been to the location. You have a sketch and your iPhone photos to remind you where everything is. How many shots do you need to properly 'cover' Sc. 16? Try to visualize the finished film. Is it just one long, wide shot following the car as it stops and holding on the actor leaving the car and going into the building? Or is it several shots?

To really 'cover' this scene, maybe you need the following;

- MAS/WS — Entire Action
- LO-ANG — Car stops, door opens
- MS — Actor out of the car, looks at building.
- MCU — Action as above. Expression on Actor's face.
- ECU — The gun in Actor's hand.

- REV TRUCK — Actor runs through gap in fence.
- TRUCK — Actor runs towards building/door.
- POV/TRUCK — Running towards building/door.
- TRACK — Actor runs L – R towards building/door.
- CU — Actor's foot kicks open door.
- TOP — Actor kicks open door and goes inside building.
- LS — Entire action.

30 minutes to film this scene, remember. Probably best to keep it down to three shots. Four at the most. Maybe this way would be better…

- LO-ANGLE — Car in, Actor out, PAN to follow
- REV TRUCK — Actor runs towards building door
- MS — Actor kicks open door, goes inside
- CU — Actor's foot kicks open door.

Yes, that seems to take care of it. Four solid action-filled shots that 'cover' the scene well enough to be confident there will be some editorial leeway.

But wait – don't fall into the Trust Trap. Never take other people's work for granted and assume everything is under control. You'd better take a look at Scs. 89 & 91 and hope nobody messed up because if the additional scenes are longer than calculated — or if they are so technically-challenging they can't be shot in the allotted time — then you have a problem. The most egregious being that there's no way your crew is going to enjoy that 8.30 a.m. breakfast.

We know that we have to shoot Scenes 89 and 90 at this location and on the same day — so let's check them out now. Your UPM and/or A.D. squeezed your Time into a pre-determined Page/Shoot ratio. If they lack experience or didn't fully consider the challenges of the scenes — you might have been hung out on a limb. Perhaps they looked at the scenes, saw some potential issues, but are optimistic about your chances of 'making the day'. Remember, nobody else is thinking about how to shoot these scenes the way that you must. Other Department Heads will have looked closely at the three scenes scheduled, but few of them are considering the Time it will take to shoot them. They're thinking things like;

'Do I need extra hair spray for these scenes? Did the director tell me what color of shirt Jack is wearing? Is the gun a revolver or a semi-auto? What time should Craft Service be called? Where will we put the generator? Can I get a tax write-off on my new Ferrari if I substitute it for the BMW and rent it back to the production?'

You, my director friend, are holding the baby.

```
89. EXT. ABANDONED FACTORY. DAY.

HELEN's face is bruised and bloodied. She stag-
gers out of the building, holding onto PIERCE
for support. He looks around wildly…

                    PIERCE
          Where is he? Where the hell
          is he?!

HELEN slumps. PIERCE struggles to hold her up-
right and carry her away from the building.
```

Good. Not too much action. It looks more like 2/8th but no matter. Probably do this in a single shot. Add another Set-up to get some coverage. Have to make sure that HELEN is in the Make-up chair in plenty of time so we're not hanging around waiting for her to be 'bruised and bloodied'. Add this to Sc. 16 and we've got 3/8ths. Yes! Scs. 16 and 89 can be shot out in an hour. No problem! I love my U.P.M and/or 1st A.D. They're totally professional. They're looking out for their director. We'll be having breakfast at 8.30!

Now, what about Sc. 91?

91. EXT. ABANDONED FACTORY. DAWN.

The TRUCK swings off the road at high speed, smashes through the chain-link fence, side-swipes the dumpsters and skids to a stop. JACK jumps out and runs to help PIERCE as he half-drags, half-carries HELEN to safety.

                    JACK
          What happened?

                    PIERCE
          Later! We've got to get her
          out of here!

JACK helps PIERCE lift HELEN into the truck. The men climb in after her, Jack behind the wheel. He slams into gear and the truck takes off, crashing through another section of the fence. Bouncing crazily out onto the road, tires screeching, the truck roars away.

What the...!!! Those fools! Call themselves professionals? U.P.M and/or 1st A.D? Don't make me laugh! Who hired these brain-dead carrion crows? How can anyone shoot this kind of material, and two additional scenes, in 2 hours?!

It's clear that your U.P.M and/or 1st A.D. will have to die horribly for doing this to you. You've been given what looks like another 4/8ths to shoot and an hour to do so — but this last scene is complicated. A truck has to go through a fence! Not once — twice! Working fast, it may take two hours to shoot, possibly two and a half given the stunt driving work, and only if your stunt and camera crews are organized. In terms of action and excitement Scs. 16 & 81 don't hold much importance now, do they? Okay, we'll get over our tantrum and on with the job.

There's some good news. The Line Producer realized Sc. 91 would be tough to accomplish in the time frame. He thinks you can shoot the truck in/truck out stunt sequences in one take each, so he budgeted for a second camera, which your 1st Assistant Camera will operate. What a prince!

You have to shoot Sc. 16 first, because the script calls for a DAWN shot. It can't be shifted to regular daylight without changing the tone and continuity. The scene comes early in the script, so you need to establish the location clearly so the audience will remember where they are when they see Scs. 89 & 91 later. And you have to be quick. There's a trick often used in 'action' films made for under $100,000. You shoot the entire scene using a dolly and track — because once the track is down, the time-consuming work is done. You keep the camera on the dolly — moving it wherever you want. You block the action so that you can shoot a Master from the dolly and get all kinds of angles, plus movement. If you need smooth fast motion — you have the optimum camera support. Lastly, it's faster to change lenses than it is to move a camera and tripod to a fresh position. Lens changes give you shot variety in minimal time. How about this as your first Set-up/Shot for Sc. 16?

TRACKING (fast, L – R) along the 'sagging perimeter fence' as the BMW screeches up to the curb and Jack jumps out.

That's what came into my 'vision'. Your internal movie screen might see something very different. That's okay. Whatever that 'vision' is, you need to consider it before you commit. My consideration of this potential Set-up tells me that lots of good things might happen…

- Movement: Film is about motion. JACK is in a hurry. The BMW comes in fast. On track, the camera can move fast too. The fence slicing by in the foreground (f.g.) will increase the sense of momentum.

- Economy: One of the interesting things about feature-film making, as opposed to television, commercials, music videos and the like, is that you can do a lot with one shot because of the amount of information, action and understanding you can put into your frame. Sometimes you don't even realize, until it's done, that the shot you just made actually does everything that is required — that there is no need to add anything more. If you deliberately look to economize, then you automatically start creating strong, information-packed images.

- Sub-Text: That fence in the foreground might suggest that, at this moment in our story, JACK is on the 'other side'. He hasn't yet crossed an invisible line that will take him into the next level of the story. Into danger perhaps, or a life-altering moment. Given that this is Sc. 16, it's likely the point in the film where Jack has accepted what screenwriters who follow the precepts of the 'Hero's Journey' term, the 'Call To Adventure'. Something has happened, or is *about* to happen, to propel the story forward and keep the audience engaged.

- Image System: You might be creating a System. Maybe fences, or barriers of every kind, are present throughout the film in subtle and not so subtle ways. Maybe JACK's story arc is that he's always coming up against obstacles. Maybe crashing through the fence in Sc. 91 further on in the movie will be indicative of how far he has 'arced' and how powerful his character has become.

Okay, let's commit to the idea and start to build.

Scene 16: Shot #1/ Set-Up #1

WS/TRACK (fast, L to R), Fence in f.g., as BMW enters/stops. JACK runs thru gap in fence, leaves frame CAM R.

There's a 'hidden' problem here that isn't quite resolved yet — but we'll visit that later. Oh — and here's a location diagram with the BMW's first and final positions laid out...

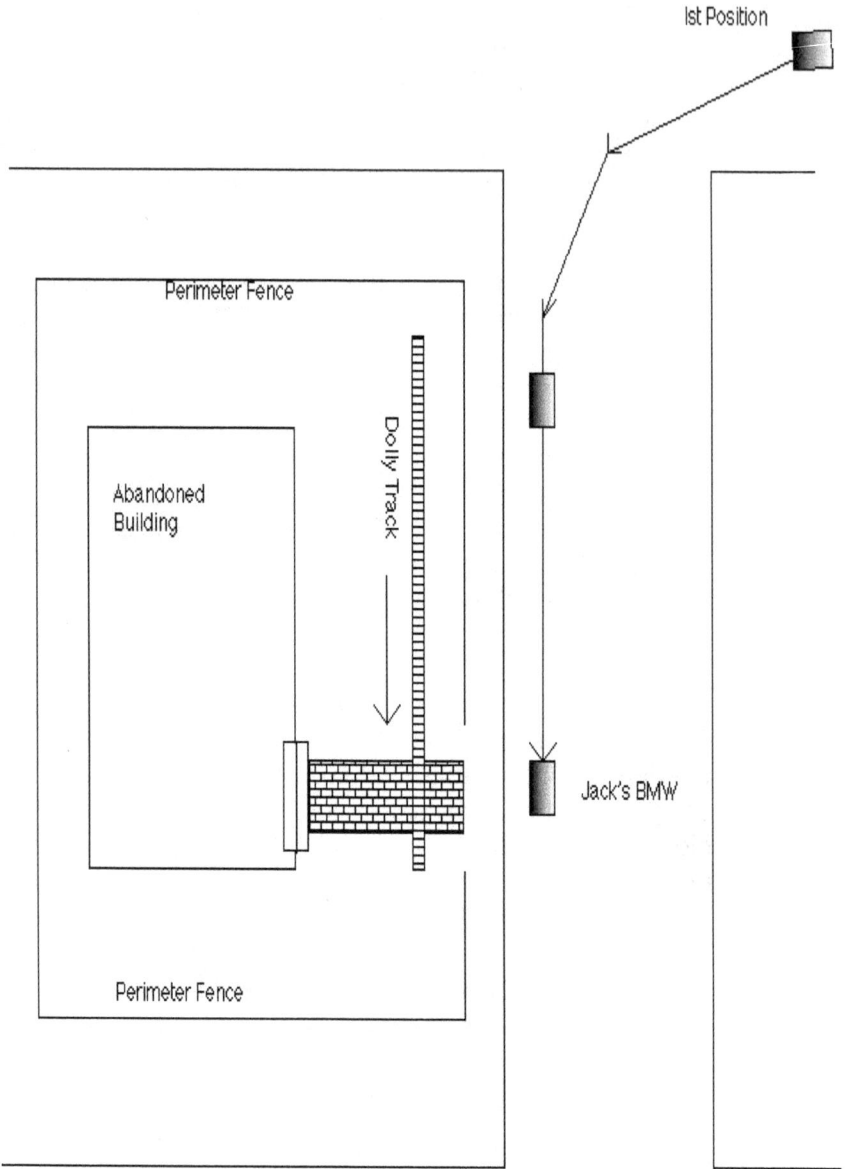

1st Position

Perimeter Fence

Dolly Track

Abandoned
Building

Jack's BMW

Perimeter Fence

Location Diagram, Sc. 16

We're in the business of saving Time. Once the awe-some tracking shot of the BMW arriving is done, and Jack has passed camera on the way to the building, we simply — RE-VERSE! Keep the camera on the track. Just spin it around and pick up JACK as he runs past the camera. You could stay in WS if you like, but you might fully establish the GUN if you start Shot #2 in MCU or CU and let JACK move progressively away into FS then LS until he kicks open the door and disappears in-side the building. A good 1st A.C. will be able 'follow' JACK with the focus all the way from CU to LS. By keeping LO-ANG to catch the GUN in CU as JACK runs up and goes by, (making a 180° PAN as he passes), we will see the building looming ominously above him, giving the sense that he is being dwarfed by the structure.

And there's your scene in two shots. By making Shot #2 in this way, you've actually accomplished two shots in one — the CU of the GUN, and the EST/LS of JACK running towards the building. Producers love directors who can do this. Notate!

<u>Sc. 16 Shot #2/Set-Up #2</u>

REVERSE/FIXED/LO-ANGLE w/PAN. CU on GUN, PAN L-R and follow focus to FS/LS as JACK runs to bldg. and enters.

Two Shots down, one scene shot, two scenes to go. Time has forced you to be economical. It has forced you to grab all the Sc. 16 information in two powerful shots. It has forced you to make the change from Set-up #1 to Set-up #2 in the smallest amount of time.

All right, next....

89. EXT. ABANDONED FACTORY. DAY.

HELEN's face is bruised and bloodied. She stag-gers out of the building, holding onto PIERCE for support. He looks around wildly…

>   PIERCE
>   Where is he? Where the hell
>   is he?!

HELEN slumps. PIERCE struggles to hold her upright and carry her away from the building.

That door that JACK went through in Sc. 16? Well, HELEN and PIERCE are going to come out of it in Sc. 89. If you take a look at the Location Diagram you could stay on the dolly, find an angle and lens that works and quickly shoot the scene. You could… but you might get a better shot HAND-HELD or think it better to go with STICKS for an angle that reveals more information and gives you a better 2-SHOT as the actors come out of the building.

But wait, there's something else. While HELEN and PIERCE are in MUAH, you still have JACK on-set — and you really do need a closer shot of him kicking open that door and going into the building…. If camera and lighting are going to be reset for Sc. 89, everything will be in approximately the right place to grab a new angle of JACK kicking open that door.

Sc. 16 Shot #3/ Set-Up #3

STICKS/MCU/ LO-ANGLE. JACK runs in from Cam L, kicks open door and goes into building.

Sc. 16 is complete in three shots. Make a fast and minor re-set for Sc. 89. PIERCE & HELEN arrive on-set for the 'walk-thru' and are 'blocked' for their scene.

Sc. 89. Shot #1/ Set-Up #4 and Shot #2/Set-Up #5

H/H/MS. PIERCE & HELEN exit bldg. Line delivery, out CAM R
H/H MCU. Same action, out CAM R

And so, with economy and efficiency, you have 'shot out' both Sc. 16 and Sc. 89 in 5 shots. With 'coverage'.

However, I have laid a small glitch in our scenario example. You'll have noticed that we jump from Sc. 89 to Sc. 91 and, very unfairly, I have not indicated what happens in Sc. 90. If you will accept that no screenwriter would have written the 'missing' scene to be more than a quick cutaway (Jack driving the truck/the villain giving chase) then the temporal shift between Sc. 89 and Sc. 91 will be minor. But what if it's not?

What often happens as you work through a Shot List — and, again, it's another good reason to go through the discipline of building a List — is that you notice a continuity or editorial issue. In this case, Sc. 89 needs to connect with Sc. 91. By looking at the scene between the two — Sc. 90 — you'll know how long that gap is in terms of 'Story Time'. The question becomes; *'If we leave Pierce and Helen at the tail of Sc. 89 as simply disappearing out of frame, then where are they at the start of Sc. 91'?*

I mention this because when you build a List, you have to consider the next scene. You have to decide how you will leave the current scene and transition into the next. If it turns out that Sc. 90 is a quick cutaway to JACK in the truck, pedal to the metal, then you could leave HELEN and PIERCE fully in frame, HELEN in a faint, PIERCE manfully holding onto her. But if Sc.90 takes us away from HELEN and PIERCE for more than a moment, then we can't leave them standing outside the building, only to discover them in exactly the same spot when we return. It's at this moment that you wonder if Sc. 90 is necessary. Surely a hard cut from PIERCE and HELEN in Sc. 89 to the truck crashing through the fence at the start of Sc. 91 would be effective. Would it make sense to delete Sc. 90, or put it somewhere else, and merge Sc. 91 into Sc. 89? You're the director. Those are your decisions, and those are the kind of questions you find yourself asking if you take the trouble to Shot List.

If Sc.90, whatever its length, stays — here would be my solution to a temporal and spatial problem that the writer didn't fully notice. A solution that will work whether Sc.90 is brief, long or left on the (virtual) cutting room floor. My solution? I don't 'leave' Sc. 89 until I have made a 3rd Shot.

Sc. 89. Shot #3/ Set-Up #6

REVERSE/MS to FS, establish Perimeter Fence in b.g, PIERCE and HELEN enter from CAM L walk into FS and collapse.

This is a seamless 'cut' from Sc. 89's Shot #2, the frontal angle on HELEN and PIERCE that had them leave frame CAM R. By reversing the shot, the fence is established in the background — an important reminder for the audience. If Pierce struggles to hold Helen and the pair 'collapse' to the ground, I've got them 'fixed' in space. They're in a good place, no matter if Sc. 91 doesn't arrive for 3 seconds or 3 minutes. If the 'missing' scene is deleted at a later date, it's still good.

- *'Really? How can you cut to the truck coming through the fence in Sc. 91 if, in the previous shot, the audience can clearly see the fence and the empty roadway beyond Pierce and Helen? Your 'Reverse', Mr. Innocenti, won't work if Sc. 90 is deleted.'*

So glad you brought that up and, of course, you are correct. Shot Listing. Gotta love it. Always revealing little flaws in the plan... and at a moment when there's still time to fix them.

You didn't think we were going straight to the big 'truck-thru-the-fence' moment, did you? Nay, nay and thrice nay. We're going to solve the problem you've raised and spend some time getting worthwhile shots while our hard-working crew is given an opportunity to prepare our Truck Stunt Extravaganza.

Here's the first two shots for Sc. 91;

Sc. 91. Shot #1/ Set-Up #7

MCU/2SH/EYE/BABY LEGS. PIERCE reacts (to off-screen (o/s) truck arrival) and struggles to help HELEN up.

Sc. 91. Shot #2/Set-Up #8

MS/2SH/STICKS. Reaction and rise. PIERCE delivers line. JACK enters CAM R and helps support HELEN. All leave frame CAM R. *Watch for 180°.*

Let's remind ourselves of what is going on here.

```
91. EXT. ABANDONED FACTORY. DAWN.

The TRUCK swings off the road at high speed,
smashes through the chain-link fence, side-
swipes the dumpsters and skids to a stop. JACK
jumps out and runs to help PIERCE as he half-
drags, half-carries HELEN to safety.

                    JACK
          What happened?

                    PIERCE
          Later! We've got to get her
          out of here!

JACK helps PIERCE lift HELEN into the truck.
The men climb in after her, Jack behind the
wheel. He slams into gear and the truck takes
off, crashing through another section of the
fence. Bouncing crazily out onto the road,
tires screeching, the truck roars away.
```

It is not incumbent on you to precisely follow the manner in which the Screenwriter has laid out the linear action of the scene. The Writer has not made PIERCE and HELEN's situation/condition the opening of Sc. 91. In fact, there is no written description of Pierce having a reaction to the truck coming through the fence at all. Technically, a Director could follow the strict guidelines presented in the script — but as Director you are now, in a very real sense, retelling the story that you "heard" from the Writer to a third party — the audience. And every storyteller recounts a tale in a slightly different manner, with different emphasis and shading — sometimes with different outcomes. As a storyteller, I'm interested in Pierce's reaction because I sense he's an important character and because I think it will be interesting to see both surprise and relief on his face when that truck blasts through the fence.

Pierce has one line in Sc. 91 — a response to Jake's *'what happened?'* question. By shooting his dialogue line, we've jumped out of continuity and now we're assembling pieces of footage for the edit room.

But what have these two shots accomplished? First, we've 'extended' the tail of Sc.89. Last time we saw Pierce and Helen, they were "collapsed" on the ground with their backs to us and the 'empty' fence in the b.g. The two shots we've just made reverse that. They are 'frontal' and because they include Pierce's 'reaction' to the truck coming through the fence, whether Sc. 90 is shot or deleted now makes no difference. We are 'covered'.

But, there's more. In terms of production efficiency, shooting 'away' from the fence lets the crew (Art Dept., in particular) keep working. They've probably been setting up for Sc. 91 from the moment they arrived, prepping the fence and the truck. The Grips have been busy getting the camera positions ready. They've dug and sand-bagged a shallow pit close to the dumpsters so as to place the 'B' camera in a position where the fence will come down directly into frame and the truck roar over the position. The Stunt Coordinator will have checked the ground, the fence, the truck, the angles and the issues of safety. The Stunt Driver will be in Costume and MUAH being made to approximate 'Jack'. That's not all. As soon as the camera was lifted off the dolly to go and shoot Sc. 89, they moved the track 90°. At your direction, naturally.

1st Position

Perimeter Fence

Abandoned
Building

Truck

B

A

Dolly Track

Perimeter Fence

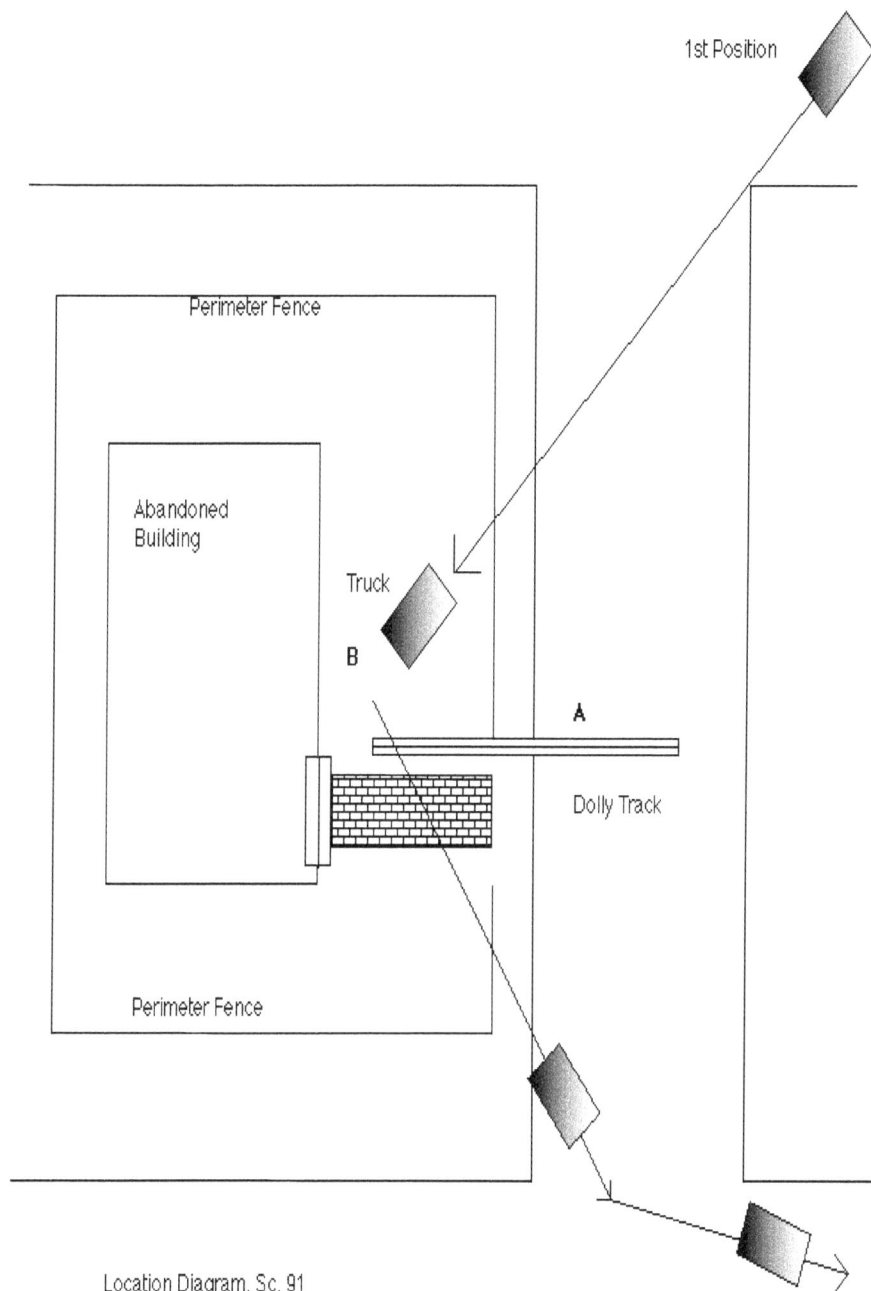

Location Diagram, Sc. 91

The diagram for Sc. 91 shows the approximate positioning of the truck's 'entry' and 'exit' and the new position for the track — extending into the roadway and through a gap in the fence created by the Art Dept. The 'A' camera is on the dolly/track. In reality, the position for the 'B' camera would be closer to point of truck/fence impact than the diagram shows.

Given that shooting has continued while the 'work' was going on behind us, we've already got an important angle, and 2 shots completed. Looking at the diagram, and with reference to the script, you might like to consider the next shots you'd make in this situation. (And don't think you have to keep the dolly and track — or even use the 'B' camera as a 'crash cam'. In fact, if you're shooting 4K Digital you'd likely be using a bunch of inexpensive 'crash cams' located in, on and around the truck and the point(s) of impact). I'm going to keep working with only 2 cameras for this exercise, and assume the 'B' Camera, though cheaper and less fancy, still needs to be protected.

Here's my plan; 'A' Camera on the dolly at the far right of the track, per the diagram. With the first position in the roadway, we will be able to fast track with the truck from the road, be at 90° to it as it jumps the curb, and follow as it crashes through the fence, sideswipes the dumpsters and grinds to a stop. I will use the entire length of the track to get the shot. That's my 'concept'. Is it efficient? Is it powerful? Does it have significant motion? Will it get me 'coverage'? I think so.

Sc. 91. Shot #3/ Set-Up #9, Shot #4/Set-Up #10

CAM A/MAS-FS/TRACK R-L follow truck from road thru fence
CAM B/MS/FIXED/LO-ANG on truck thru' fence to stop

Two Set-ups, and two camera positions, to get the (stunt) truck into the yard where it comes to a crunching halt. Will those two shots be enough? Will everything come together in a single perfect take? Will there be a chance for a second take? A third take? Not according to our Time Allotment and our 'Micro-Budget'. If you discover that uncomfortable truth in

Shot Listing, rather than on-set or in the edit room, you'll have given yourself the opportunity to buy more time, or lobby for the additional cameras you need for the 'moment'. Yet another fine reason to Shot List. I'm losing count of all these marvelous advantages!

Everyone is feeling mighty pleased with themselves now that the Big Truck Moment has been captured for posterity. But now you've got to get Jack out of the truck and run to help Pierce help Helen to the truck, then help Helen into the truck. Then Pierce has to clamber into the truck, while Jack has to run around to the driver's side to get behind the wheel....

I think it was Editor Thelma Schoonmaker who called this 'Shoe Leather'. As a Director, finding ways to avoid actors doing mundane things is going to be a lifetime of challenge. When in doubt, cut it out, or shoot it in bite-size pieces that can be edited to make the Travel Time short and keep energy in your scene. Remember Mr. Hitchcock's maxim; *'Film is real life, with the boring bits cut out'*.

We've completed the first Big Shot of the truck thru' the fence. Momentum must be maintained. The 'A' Camera is still on the dolly & track and it's pointing in the right direction. A quick change of lens and you could easily grab a MASTER LONG shot to 'cover' the action of JACK leaping out of the truck and running to help PIERCE and HELEN who stagger towards him. Keep shooting until the trio get into the truck. Using wireless lavalier mics, you will also be able to capture the dialogue and the actors' exertion efforts.

Sc. 91. Shot #5/ Set-Up #11

LS/TRACK complete action. JACK out of truck, to ALL in truck.

This is a shot that 'stands back' from the action and observes. It is 'coverage'… and more. You've already got the head of the scene, with PIERCE and his reaction, including his dialogue response to JACK's 'What happened?' line. In this shot, you will get Jack's line 'on camera' for the first time. However, Shot #5, being LONG, might not seem to maintain the intensity of the previous shots because it holds the entire 'Shoe Leather' action and Mr. Hitchcock's boring bits don't get cut out. Nevertheless, this kind of partial MASTER of a scene is technically useful, as we shall see. Another benefit of making this shot is because — framed well, and at the correct distance from the action — there is a very interesting creative aspect in a LONG observational shot. In this instance, it creates a sense of little people struggling against the big, bad world. That might be very effective in the story line the script is suggesting.

Further, keeping the camera on the dolly & track for Shot #5 doesn't just save time — there's yet another creative element as there always should be whenever camera movement is present. The Innocenti watchword of the day is; *No motion without a notion*. So, what's the 'notion' that will justify me moving the camera? Well, if this shot is used in the final edited sequence, it will come immediately after the excitement and rapid movement of the 'Truck Stunt'. Given the distance from the action, this LS will have a slow, almost dreamlike movement to it (first from R to L as Jack jumps out and runs towards Pierce/Helen, and then L to R as they go to the truck —ending with a good angle of Jack getting behind the wheel).

It's a camera movement that gives a nice breathing space after the 'stunt' and a subtle ratcheting-up of tension. As you creep the camera along the track, watching our characters stumble and stagger towards the waiting truck, the voices inside the audience's heads are screaming; *"Hurry up! Get out of there! Move faster!"*

The more I think... the more I like!

Time is getting short. The crew are repositioning the 'B' camera for the 2nd Truck thru' fence. It's at this moment when you could — with confidence — go to a final 2-camera Set-Up and drive your cast and the truck out of Sc. 91. And this is what I like about Shot Listing. It gives me an opportunity to outline both my minimum and maximum requirements. If things go sideways, a Shot List prevents panic because it will give me an escape route if I have to find a way to wrap a scene up in as quick and tidy a manner as possible. So, right here I'd probably draw a dotted line that told me that as long as I made the final 'truck thru' fence' shots the crew are prepping, I could I leave the location knowing that I had 'covered' all three scenes well enough to live another day.

But let's pretend that things went swimmingly and there's still time on the clock. Or maybe something serendipitous happened — like the UPM coming onto the set looking worried, and whispering to me that the caterers turned up late — and breakfast won't be ready until 9 a.m.

With time in hand, you don't have to go to the final shot(s) immediately. So, you consult the shots below that dotted line, and see how many of them you can do before it becomes necessary to go the final 'truck/fence' moment. It's now about prioritizing — identifying if there's an important piece missing. We've had a MS and MCU of Pierce's line, but Jack's line only exists in the FS. Also, the 'shoe leather' section of the trio getting into the truck ideally needs more footage. So, let's remind ourselves what needs more work.

```
JACK jumps out and runs to help PIERCE as he
half-drags, half-carries HELEN to safety.

                    JACK
          What happened?

                    PIERCE (O/S)
          Later! We've got to get her
          out of here!

JACK helps PIERCE lift HELEN into the truck.
The men climb in after her, Jack behind the
wheel.
```

We've already shot Pierce's side of the dialogue, (and I've marked his line (O/S) for clarity). When the Shot I'm planning (Shot #6) is made, Jack will start in the truck, and run towards camera, while Helen and Pierce will wait behind camera. Although he's o/s when Jack delivers his line, Pierce will respond— and the sound mixer will record the o/s line.

Sc. 91. Shot #6/ Set-Up #12

FS to MS. JACK out of truck, runs towards CAM L, delivers line, leaves frame CAM L. Re-enters CAM L with PIERCE & HELEN — all go to truck. *Watch for 180°.*

This is a shot that has Jack, in FULL running towards camera into MEDIUM, delivering his line presumably as he's moving. Which means the 1st Assistant Camera is 'pulling focus' to follow the action, then reversing the 'pull' as the trio re-enter frame and run to the truck. It may take a couple of takes, but once it's done there is now additional COVERAGE of Sc. 91.

You now have three separate shots for the edit;

Shot #2: (MS; Helen & Pierce, including Pierce dialogue),
Shot #5: (TRACK/FS; Complete action, with all dialogue)
Shot #6: (FS/MS; Jack, with dialogue, and ALL to truck)

Congratulations. You are a 'Master of Shoe Leather Removal'

• *Watch for 180°? What's that about?*

Well-noticed. Take another look at the Listings for Shot#2 and Shot #6;

(Shot #2) MS/2-SHOT/STICKS. Reaction and rise. PIERCE delivers line. JACK <u>enters CAM R</u> and helps support HELEN. <u>All leave frame CAM R.</u> *Watch for 180°.*

(Shot #6) FS to MS. JACK out of truck, runs towards CAM L, delivers line, <u>leaves frame CAM L. Re-enters CAM L</u> with PIERCE & HELEN — all go to truck. *Watch for 180°.*

The editor will be cutting between these two shots, both of which have actors delivering lines to each other and — more importantly — moving out of, and back into, frame. In the heat of production, especially when the shots don't follow on from each other during shooting, the best of us can become forgetful or confused.

'Watch For 180°' is a reminder to myself not to 'Cross The Line' and break the 180° Rule.

Uh-oh.

CHAPTER FIVE

Crossing The Line

You can't spend time of film sets without encountering the 180° Rule sooner or later. It's one of those things that can lead to disagreements, cursing and time-wasting. Cinematographers and Script Supervisors live by the Rule and are usually the best arbiters if a problem or concern should arise. But truth be told, even these professionals, familiar as they are with the Rule, sometimes get it wrong.

To illustrate. A few years ago, I was directing a 'spec' commercial that included 'wire-work' with the cast and stunt crew. We were shooting in Long Beach on the former ocean-liner Queen Mary (built, as I was, in Glasgow, Scotland). In a martial arts fight sequence, one of the cast jumps over a railing on the top deck and lands on the deck below (thus, the 'wire' stunt). Earlier in our night shoot, we had shot the 'landing' on the lower deck. Now, late at night, we had filmed the fight on the upper deck and were about to shoot the 'jump' over the rail. We set up the camera… and I realized that we were about to break The 180° Rule. I mentioned this to the Cinematographer, one of my dearest long-time friends, and he said I was wrong. Definitely. Conclusively. Prove-ably. A younger Director would perhaps have accepted this — especially as, in this case, the Cinematographer was also an eminent teacher of the subject at prestigious film schools.

My Cinematographer friend and I are not the kind of people to get upset or worked up when our viewpoints differ. After all, it's only a movie — and we enjoy a good argument. Gradually, the entire crew chimed in, each one positing a viewpoint, and I allowed a relaxing moment of downtime while opinions were expressed. Eventually, I took the set photographer's camera and shot some still frames with the actor to prove my point — thus ending the discussion before the outbreak of democracy got out of hand. Obviously, those who sided with our Cinematographer were as tired as he was. In those moments when you've been working for hours, and what has already been shot becomes a jumble of half-remembered images, it's very easy to think through a problem incorrectly. To make matters worse, the tired brain will continue to insist that your (wrong) decision is correct — even in the face of contrary evidence.

So, allow me to define this 180° Rule, at the risk of either being boringly simplistic, or excruciatingly unclear. We'll go over this again later in the series when we're dealing with Actors and their Eyelines, because the point has to be hammered home. 'Crossing The Line' is something that can happen to the best of us and you need to have a good understanding of it.

Film works because of a juxtaposition of images. But what 'connects' our images? Using *The Missing Link* as an example and cutting between a couple of random CLEAN SINGLE shots of Michael King as 'Grog' and K.C. Morgan as 'Patrick', the audience accepts only that they're looking at 'Grog' one moment, and 'Patrick' the next. There may be no definitive reason to suppose that the two shots are connected in the same physical space or in the same time frame, even though they might be similar in size, with similar tonal qualities, lighting etc.

If you want to 'connect' 'Grog' and 'Patrick' in the audience's mind — connect them in the same general space at the same general time and, further, if that 'connection' is

something they, as characters, both understand and see —
then you have to let the audience know that they are, in fact,
aware of each other. Filmmakers make this connection between 'Grog' and 'Patrick' by placing an invisible straight Line
between them. Once that invisible Line has been established,
the camera is kept on one side of it, and does not cross over to
the other side. Not without taking the audience very obviously,
very clearly and very understandably 'over' The Line.

If you were to film everything in shots wide enough to
frame both characters, this tyrannical straight line would be unnecessary, because the audience would be able to see both
characters at all times and know where the characters were in
relation to each other without any difficulty.

When in doubt, sketch a Top Shot, or Bird's Eye View
of your characters and connect them with a straight line.

That Line (or Lines in the case of multiple characters) becomes the 180° that you *cannot* cross over. You can place the camera on *either* side of The Line, but ALL your shots have to stay on that side of The Line (with certain exceptions). You can be as close to The Line or as far away from The Line as you wish, but you must *never* cross over it.

The Line is as straight as 180° and rigid as a metal bar, which is why it is sometimes referred to as 'The Iron'.

Film isn't like a stage play where the audience sits and sees the whole thing unfold in front of them through a proscenium arch — in essence, a single shot of fixed size. Film uses a variety of framing sizes, which has the unfortunate yet intriguing result of character(s) being alone onscreen even though we know that there are other character(s) present.

CAM LEFT   CAM RIGHT

If we stay on the correct side of The Line already established in the MASTER 2-SHOT on the previous page, then 'Grog' will be looking out of Camera Left when he talks to 'Patrick'… and our S/C of 'Patrick' will have him engaging with 'Grog' by looking out of Camera Right.

CAM LEFT   CAM RIGHT

In these Clean Single examples above, I've gone right up to the Line. There's not much room, judging from these frames, to go any closer — but there's a whole lot of room to step back from the Line and shoot more oblique angles, had I wanted that. But no matter where I put the camera, as long as I don't 'go over' The Line, then 'Patrick' will continue to engage 'Grog' with an eyeline going out of Camera Right, and 'Grog' will have an eyeline towards Camera Left.

But let's say I shot Grog's Single then 'Crossed The Line' inadvertently to shoot Patrick's S/C. I didn't, but you'll see what I mean if I flip the image horizontally...

... and when we cut back to Grog...

Uncomfortable, isn't it? Both our characters are looking towards Camera Left. And not at each other. The audience is now confused. Hopefully, you are not.

There's usually a day in my week where I have lunch with some old friends. I emphasize 'old', for indeed we are a bunch of *alta kockers* all of whom have worked, or still work, in the Los Angeles film industry.

So, I bring up the 180° Rule in the presence of two Film Directors and a Screenwriter. Interesting discussions ensued. Nobody agreed with me that the 180° Rule was important for the reasons I have outlined in this chapter. One of the Directors (seven feature films, multiple 'major-studio' screenplays) said that whenever The Line is being questioned, arguments usually break out between the Director of Photography and the Script Supervisor — and his way of dealing with the issue is always to shoot it both ways. It's quicker, it mollifies everybody, and the Editor can decide. He then suggested, and this was agreed by the others, that even if an audience noticed that The Line had been 'crossed', they would either compensate for it because they understood that the camera had merely moved to a different angle, or they wouldn't care. The example given was the way in which football used to be broadcast with the cameras never moving from one side of the field (thus not 'crossing the line'), until an innovation was introduced — and a single camera started to be used on the opposite side. When that technique was first broadcast, a 'super' would inform the audience that they were now looking at an 'opposite angle'. Quaint, wasn't it? In today's world, audiences understand that the camera can be anywhere — in fact, they demand it — so they don't need to be told anymore with a 'super'. The same principle, my friend's argument went, applies to feature-films and cutting-edge television.

The other Director in our Gang of Four was sitting opposite me. He is also a highly-credited Editor of features and Network television, so I expected immediate confirmation that the 180° Rule was vitally important. I got a 'reality-shift' when he said that it was entirely unimportant — provided the audience remained engaged in the film and were not 'taken out of the picture'. The only Rule, as far as my friend was concerned, was that the audience should not be jolted out of the immersion. At which point, the Director to my left argued that even that 'rule' was not sacrosanct as there was often a case to disorientate the audience by crossing The Line deliberately. I had to admit that is true — you'll find it in the work of masters like Kubrick and Godard. (But it's done for an aesthetic reason).

I brought up the point that I didn't want 'Grog' to be looking out of left screen and then cut to 'Patrick' doing the same thing. There was some shrugging of shoulders. I expected the Director/Editor to suggest that if it looked really bad one of the Shots could be 'flopped' so that it appeared 'correct' — and he did say that… but he held to the view that even something that was obviously wrong was acceptable as long as the audience didn't get jolted. Both Directors had stories of scenes shot where The Line was crossed with complete abandon, without any detriment to the picture. One story involved a Daylight Exterior scene between two characters in an alley. On the first day, the only shot they had time for was the 2-Shot Master. A week later, they got one of the OTS Dirty Singles… in a different alley. Another week went by before the scene was finished with the REVERSE OTS in yet another alley. Three shots. Three locations. Three weeks apart. The Line crossed repeatedly. Result? The scene cut together perfectly.

At this point, I began to wonder if I should be writing these books at all. You might be having the same thought. But I shall persist — because conflicting opinions and wildly different approaches are all part of the fun of filmmaking. There is no correct way. Like everything else in life, you take what you need and discard what you don't.

Did I fully agree with the arguments raised? Yes, and no. I accept an edit works, even if it is 'technically wrong', provided the audience doesn't come out of the 'immersion' or if the edit is designed to shock or unsettle the viewer. I accept that, if in doubt, then sometimes the best course is to shoot 'both ways' — the same solution that is often used when you or your actor aren't sure which of two or more performances or line-readings are 'best'. I accept that contemporary audiences are so clued-in to visual presentation that they can work out what has happened when the camera is moved to a surprising or 'strange' position. I can accept it, while still thinking that it would be better if the shots had been made properly in the first place.

You'll have noticed that my third friend, the Screenwriter, (credited on some of the best known Network television shows ever made), had been careful to keep out of these exchanges, but now he mentioned that, in Canada, The Line is known as 'The Axis'. This started a terminology debate, introducing 'The Proscenium Rule' (because it places the audience as if they are in a theatre auditorium and not 'behind the actors' on the stage), 'The Axis of Action' (which sounds very macho), and, last but not least, 'The Director's Line' — because, as it turns out, only Directors care enough about the darn 'Line' to spend their lunchtime arguing about it.

To put me firmly in my place, and to fully prove everything my friends had told me at lunch, I happened to watch the ever-excellent Kathryn Bigelow's *Zero Dark Thirty* (2012). Ms. Bigelow has been a director to watch since her 1981 feature debut *The Loveless*. Thirty-seven minutes into *Zero Dark Thirty* there's an interrogation scene, set in an ISI Detention Center, with Jessica Chastain as 'Maya' and Homayoun Ershadi as 'Hassan Ghui'. The scene lasts a couple of minutes and during it the 180° rule is broken four times. We could ask 'why'? The flippant answer might be 'why not?' The real answer lies in technique. By ignoring the 180° Rule, Ms. Bigelow and Editor William Goldenburg created an unstoppable flow and a freshness to the shots, and the order in which those shots were assembled. Whenever Ms. Bigelow establishes a Line, she adds interest not by the traditional ping-pong of matched reverses, but by deliberately choosing angles that are either very close to The Line, or obliquely distanced from it. When she Crosses The Line, it's done to ramp up interest, in effect to make the audience sit up and listen — to understand that the question 'Maya' is asking, or the answer 'Hassan' gives, is important. The technique also adds tension — there is nothing flat about the scene, not just because the actors are superb, but also because the camera and the edit are 'active'. The editorial flow of the scene is perfect *because* The Line is being crossed. There is a safety net, of course — the characters are sitting opposite each other so we already know their exact spatial relationship — but, because of that, the director can confidently throw away the 180° Rule and break the convention to heighten the scene. Rather like a jazz trumpet player hitting a discordant note to get the attention and adulation of the hep-cats — if you'll forgive my tendency towards music analogies.

So. That's the 180°. I still think it's important and, at minimum, I'd like you to be able to argue with your Director of Photography and/or Script Supervisor, should the need arise, with a degree of confidence.

When we revisit the 180° again in a future series title, it will be to fully understand 'eyeline' direction so you can guide your Actors. We'll also explore ways to shoot multiple characters, especially in confined spaces, without making your Editor or audience displeased, or having your head explode — because once you have multiple characters in a scene… this nonsense gets real.

Oh, did I mention the 30° Rule? Yes, there's another one. We'll discuss that when we get to Editing. For now, we will return to Sc. 91 and the *'Watch for 180°'* note that brought us here.

CHAPTER SIX

Back to the Build

Shot #2 was shot 'out of continuity' while the crew were busy setting up the Big Truck Action. Four Set-Ups later we come back for Shot #6 to get the 'other side' of the sequence.

(Shot #2) MS/2-SHOT/STICKS. Reaction and rise. PIERCE delivers line. JACK <u>enters CAM R</u> and helps support HELEN. <u>All leave frame CAM R.</u> *Watch for 180°.*

(Shot #6) FS to MS. JACK out of truck, runs towards CAM L, delivers line, <u>leaves frame CAM L.</u> <u>Re-enters CAM L</u> with PIERCE & HELEN — all go to truck. *Watch for 180°.*

All we have to remember is that, to maintain the 180°, eyelines and actors that have gone out of (or entered from) Camera *Right* in Shot #2, should exit or enter Camera *Left* In Shot #6. As long as you've established where the Line is and obey the Rule, your actors will have correct eyelines and will enter and leave frames in such a way that additional shots from different angles will cut together.

If they do not – if Jack walks out on Camera Right (Shot #6) and we see him entering Camera Right in the next shot (in the edited sequence — Shot #2) then it will appear that either Jack came from somewhere else – and we have a jump cut —

or the audience for a brief moment might think that Jack is somebody else. I know this is complicated until you get the hang of it and you might have developed a headache. A sketch can sometimes help. It doesn't matter if your drawing is incomprehensible to anyone but yourself. In this instance the important information is the dotted line between the truck and Pierce and Helen — with its visual reminder of where your camera positions should be in relation to the line.

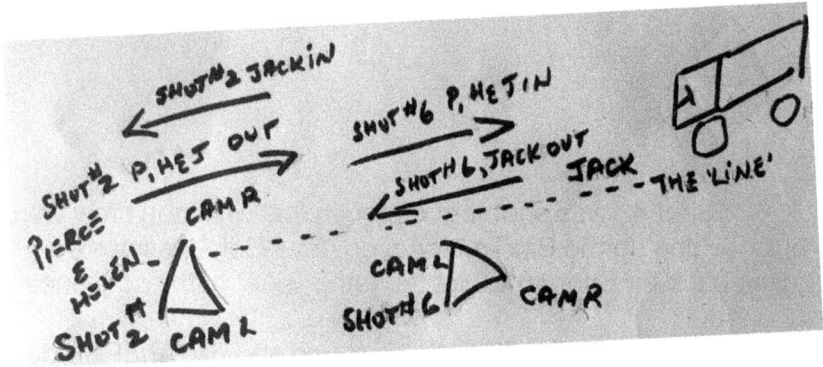

Time marches on. We have to get out of this scene and leave this location. We've already got that (slow tracking) LS of the trio going to the truck, and we've just made a MS to FS (with Focus Pull) to repeat that action. Another shot which catches them closer to the truck and watches them get aboard is a luxury in 'micro-budget' but let's live large. We want a certain frenetic tension as the trio make their escape, some urgency — so perhaps we go Hand-Held.

Sc. 91. Shot #7/ Set-Up #13

MS/MCU/H/H. JACK, PIERCE, HELEN to the truck. (Possible STEADI, or true H/H with wide-angle lens)

In Shot #7 we'll get the final moments as they arrive at the truck. The effort of helping Helen inside. Pierce clambering after her. Jack slamming the passenger door and leaving frame to go around to the driver's side and reappear behind the wheel...

Shot #7 is very useable. But to put the frosting on the cake you need a REVERSE. The Producers just stepped onto the set, wondering how it's all going. Nod confidently at them and smile. Take the H/H Camera to the other side of the truck and find an apple box — quick! — to give the camera operator enough height. Start Shot #8 on Pierce and Helen clambering into the truck, a bit of business perhaps as Pierce wipes Helen's face. Pierce's eyeline going to Jack who is still off-screen, running around the front of the truck.... then the camera swings and catches Jack as he clambers into the cab. He slams the truck into gear, and it lurches off...CUT. List it.

Sc. 91. Shot #8/ Set-Up #14

REVERSE/MS-MCU/H/H/ PIERCE/HELEN in, JACK in/out.

It's not a bad series of Shots. This is the place to draw a second dotted line. Everything between the two dotted lines is expendable. 3 Shots that we can conceivably do without — but having them elevates the entire scene. To recap, if you were in a horrible time crunch you could have stopped after Shot #5 (the LS/TRACK) knowing that you had both the dialogue and the action. There are many directors, and a greater number of low-budget producers, who would stop right there and wrap the scene with a final shot of the truck leaving.

The trouble with Shot #5's LS/TRACK is that you're making the audience watch the entire 'running-for-the-truck' action in 'real time', not 'movie time' and they may get fidgety. Shot #6, the FS/MS of Jack running in, then helping the others back to the truck, fixes some of that problem but there's still not enough in those two shots to get the urgency and kinetic energy you need before the truck makes its wild exit, which is why Shots #7 and #8 are begging to be filmed.

You and your Editor need to control Time. This is one of your primary missions as a Director. Give yourself the means to do so.

- *Surely you only need one Hand-Held angle. Shot #7? Doesn't that give all the 'coverage' required, without wasting further time getting the Reverse — Shot #8?*

Yes, and no. You'd still have adequate 'coverage if you deleted Shot #8. But there comes a point when 'coverage' isn't the goal — which is something that 'micro' and 'ultra-low' budget productions sometimes forget — and which you must not.

Making entertaining and engaging motion pictures is the goal.

But there's a less high-minded reason for continuing and making Shot #8. Not just another angle that wipes away the scourge of 'Shoe Leather' — but a shot that will get you out of trouble. Whenever you go Hand-Held things tend to get messy and you can end up with a poorly-framed documentary feel. You're probably not going to get the shot right. The audience will find the moment where your operator gets too close, and Jack's back fills the screen for 4 interminable seconds, enough to make them start questioning your directorial technique. Your operator will look sourly at you and say that either it didn't work, or it was 'okay'. 'Okay' is not good enough. Your 1st Assistant Camera will also be unsure if focus held all the way. Now it's turning into a lengthy, 'Let's-get-this-right-if-it-takes-all-day' moment. Stop it now or you'll miss breakfast. You cannot afford to use up Time getting a difficult 'luxury' shot right. Pick your battles. Move on and get the H/H REVERSE from the driver's side of the truck because having both shots gives you 'safety' in the edit — you can cut to the other side whenever you run into trouble. Besides, without the REVERSE you're only half-way there — and the additional footage is going to improve the cut and put more intensity into the edit at a moment that needs urgency.

Your Producer is looking anxious and the crew is getting hungry. But there's two more shots to do, to get the truck through the fence for the second time. The dolly & track have been wrapped and the 'B' Camera is back in a shallow trench, pointing in the direction of travel and able to capture an extreme LO-ANG as the truck passes over it, going through the fence and away. Camera 'A' — sited so it cannot be seen by Camera 'B,' — is now in the roadway, close to the point where the fence will be smashed. It will PAN R-L with the truck as it passes, holding on a final frame as the truck speeds away

Sc. 91. Shot #9/ Set-Up #15, Shot #10/Set-Up #16

CAM A/MS-WS/PAN R-L follow truck from yard to road
CAM B/MS/FIXED/LO-ANG truck passes over, thru fence

Done. Let's wrap this location and have breakfast.

Could you direct 3 scenes, with stunt elements, for a total of 16 Set-Ups in under 3 hours? That's hard, but not impossible. Can you imagine what it would be like if you didn't have a Shot List? Personally, I suspect that I'd take a full 3 hours to get footage to a standard my editor and I would find acceptable, and only by driving the crew with a lot of energy, attention and encouragement.

Of course, it will be obvious to you that the scheduling and shot listing scenario I am working with is at the lower end of 'Low-Budget'. Why am I working in this ballpark? I'm being realistic enough to suggest that your early directorial work will be on very tight budgets and if you've already conceptualized and organized your shots before you step on the set you're going to be in good shape.

The kind of pressure that requires you to shoot 7/8th's of a page with action/stunt elements in under three hours doesn't happen when you're on a large-scale studio picture. Other pressures occur in those circumstances. Time is still important, but you could easily take a whole day to do a 'Stunt Truck' scene on a large-budget Action film, and you'd better think of many more demanding and creative Set-Ups than the ones I've come up with.

Now, you might disagree with the amount or type of shots I am proposing for the above three scenes — and I should hope you do. You might want to jot down your own approach to these three scenes and see how many shots you come up with. If you can sketch your shots or describe them to an artist who can sketch them — you're really getting into the game.

I could have laid my shots out in a number of different ways, but the ones I chose were the ones that seemed best to me at the time of writing. It's a basic Shot List springing from a need to move very quickly and effectively. But it may not be what I finally end up shooting. A Shot List is not written in stone. It's a note to yourself of how you'll probably proceed.

Things change on a film set. Often for the better.

At this point, the moment when words on the page become images that transform from nebulous to concrete in one's mind, most experienced directors will know exactly how many Set-Ups are required, which lenses will be on the camera for each shot, how each shot will be composed, the rhythm of the shot, the pace of the action and the emotional intent the actors will play. You might not know all these details, but from visiting the location (which we are assuming you will have done), studying the scene and knowing the Time allocated, you are now able to write down the shots you want and the order you will do them in. This is your Shot List. Nobody else on the set has one. Oh yes, there will be plenty of people on the set thinking that *their* shot would be so much better, but they won't have gone to the trouble to have a list.

Some directors have their Shot List as a 'facing' page in their script. Others have it on a slip of paper stuffed in a pocket. It's the minimal requirement for a Director. If the crew knows you have a Shot List, they will relax and let you guide them. If they suspect, or learn, that there is no Shot List and things get out of control — then expect a mutiny. Crews need Captains.

Captains need maps.

CHAPTER SEVEN

K.I.S.S.

The title of this chapter does not refer to an American rock band whose music I have never listened to, but is an acronym for '*Keep It Simple, Stupid*' — a phrase I was constantly reminded of when I first ventured into the world of professional filmmaking — a more brutal and insensitive time than the emotionally safe working environments we enjoy today.

In this book, I've insisted that building a Shot List is a healthy and wise task to undertake — and I'm shortly going to expand on ways to make it simpler than the methodology I've already outlined.

First, I should point out that it's very easy to 'over-prepare' — particularly when you're anxious to get everything right.

One of the roads into 'over-preparedness' comes from advice given regarding 'Shooting Scripts'. I've noticed that some filmmakers, heeding this advice, have spent days assembling their Principal Photography shot-by-shot or have misinterpreted the meaning of a 'Shooting Script'. So, let's define.

There is a type of 'Shooting Script', which is sometimes called a 'Shooting Schedule', and which is predominantly used in television production. A shot will be given a number, and a description (with shot size, lens, movement and action) — and usually one or more of further pieces of information regarding; day/night/location/cast/equipment/props. For example;

Shot 21 Day Wide Shot of Paul 24mm Ext Hotel

  … all well and good. Shots continue to be listed. #22 is Paul crossing the hotel lobby. #23 is Paul in the elevator. #24 has Paul walking down a corridor. #25 Paul knocks on a door. #26 Occupant of room hears door knock. #27 Paul at door as it is opened by Occupant. #28 Paul given envelope. #29 Paul coming out of elevator into lobby….

Shot 30 Day Wide Shot of Paul 24mm Ext Hotel

  In other words, this is merely a blow-by-blow account of the shots to be made, in keeping with editorial continuity. There is nothing to suggest that Shot 21 and Shot 30 are essentially the same Set-Up with the same Actor performing an action, and then reversing that action. Kinda useless, to us, don't you think? If you followed the logic and 'continuity' of this Shooting Script/Schedule you'd exhaust your entire cast and crew in no time at all and have absolutely no 'coverage'.

  Then there's the avuncular advice that you huddle with your Cinematographer in the heady days of Pre-Production and, in loving tandem, craft out a 'Shooting Script', scene-by-scene, shot-by-shot. The people who tell you this, I suspect, have never been on a professional production — especially in the 'Low', 'Modified', 'ULB' and 'Micro' budgeted worlds. They cannot conceive that you and your Cinematographer only have a limited amount of time to meet and when you do it's for 'tech scouting' the locations or discussing how to shoot a particularly challenging sequence. You may well have had early meetings with your D.P. to talk about tone, palette, equipment and the like — but, with the exception of certain shots that you both agree are important for the film, your Cinematographer expects you to do the work of Shot Listing. If you examine the fantasy the gurus have presented, the idea is that you and the Director of Photography go through the screenplay, with the proverbial fine-tooth comb, discussing exactly what you are going to shoot — and then mark up the script. Naturally, there are apps to help you and your patient cinematographer do this work which makes one suspect that much of this "guru advice" comes from persons associated with the marketing of such apps. The apps allow you to import the original 'production locked' screenplay and then, for *every* shot you plan in *every* scene, enter Shot Number, Shot Size, how the Shot is framed, how the Shot will move, how the Shot is introduced, and the estimated duration of the Shot.

The 'takeaway' that I'm suggesting is; don't feel obliged to go into minute detail in your preparedness if what you are being confronted with isn't that hard. Obviously, if you're faced with marshalling complex equipment and the tricky movement of actors and extras — all within a 'Special World' that is created through a highly developed lighting design, very precise VFX, or any demanding stunt or physical FX/Pyro work — then you are going to have to spend weeks working it all out. But if none of that applies — if you're blocking 4 actors, a few extras, a dolly movement and a lighting change within the shot — don't kill yourself. Keep your Shot Listing concise. Less is always more, because when you have a small List of the carefully-considered Shots that can be worked through efficiently and quickly — you're setting yourself up to have enough Time to add the ideas that come to you on-set. You are giving yourself the opportunity to be creative 'in the moment'. So, don't fall into the trap of spending hours that turn into days 'prepping' for every eventuality. That's a surefire way to kill your enthusiasm and energy.

I should mention that some of the gurus seem to have misunderstood the difference between a Breakdown, a Production Schedule, a Shooting Script and a Shot List and appear to suggest that all these items are part of a single document that you will distribute to every individual in your crew. As we already know from *Selecting For Success*, this is not so.

But let me quickly outline what a 'Shooting Script' actually is in terms of full-length theatrical feature production

When the Writer submits his final version of the Screenplay and everything has been fully agreed between the interested parties (Writer/Producer/Director/Investor's Parking Valet) the screenplay is 'Locked'. If the Writer has done their job right, then the script at this point in time will have NO scene numbers, nor will it have anything that is 'directorial' such as directions to shot size, camera movement, transitions or editorial techniques. The final script will now be 'numbered' and 'locked' and becomes, in some parlance, the 'Shooting Script' and, in others, the 'Locked Script'. Thereafter, if any changes are made — such as a scene being deleted, a scene added, or dialogue changed — the script will be temporarily 'unlocked', the changes made, and the script re-saved as a 'Revised' version. In the old days when this happened, revised script pages were typed up to 'over-write' the old material and were printed on a different color paper — to then be distributed and inserted into 'locked' scripts. A first revision might be on 'blue' paper. A second on 'yellow'. A third on 'pink'. It was not unusual for a 'locked' shooting script to be multi-colored by the end of production. Today, software is capable of making any revisions in such a way that it is obvious where the revision has taken place and what it is. Thus, new dialogue might appear in 'red' with asterisks in the margin to draw attention. When a scene is deleted, the scene number will remain in the script, but the scene slug and description will be replaced with 'OMIT'. Whenever a scene is added, a new scene number will be introduced so that the 'locked' numbers, already reflected in the Breakdown and Schedule, are not affected. Thus, a new scene that follows Scene 32 will be numbered 32A and Scene 33 will be unaffected. If further scenes are placed between 32A and 33 they'll be 32B, 32C etc.

Here's a list of the various 'script' forms and production 'bibles' showing where responsibility lies. The final item — 'Lined Script' — will be described more fully in a later chapter, because it has a methodology that, applied to your Shot Listing, may save you Time.

- Screenplay. Responsibility of the Screenwriter, with over sight/input from Producer and/or Director.
- Shooting Script. Responsibility of Production Office, with input from the Director. (aka 'Locked Script').
- Breakdown. Responsibility of Production Office, usually the UPM/Line Producer/1st A.D. — Director to have oversight.
- Schedule. Responsibility of Production Office, usually the UPM/Line Producer/1st A.D. — Director to have oversight.
- Shot List. Responsibility of the Director, with input from the Cinematographer and, sometimes, the 1st A.D.
- Lined Script. Responsibility of the Script Supervisor. — Production Office and Director to have oversight.

In the spirit of K.I.S.S., there's something important to add before this chapter closes. You will have noticed that when building a Shot List, the sequence in which you make your shots is designed to keep forward momentum in production and maximize efficiency so as to neither waste time nor expend crew and cast energy needlessly.

For example, in our Sc 16 scenario it would be foolish to make the dolly shot of the BMW arriving, then haul the camera off the dolly and set up the 'kicking open the door' shot, and then return to the street to film Jack getting out of the car. Instead, you plan your Shot List to get your camera and cast to the next most logical position. This often means that you shoot everything in one direction, before you turn around and shoot the action from the opposite direction. Mostly, this has to do with lighting. Waiting for lights to be re-set because you need to turn the camera around and reposition it, will eat up time and crew energy because everything has to move — not just the lights. All the equipment and personnel who, moments ago, were standing *behind* the camera are now in the frame. If you keep bouncing back between one direction and its opposite — everyone's going to be dead on their feet by lunchtime. Unless planned for, (as we did with our original Sc. 16 dolly shot which was followed immediately with a 'reverse'), moving "forward" in a single direction before doing the 'reverses' is going to save time. Where a potential problem may arise is in 'continuity' — making sure that when you come to do the 'reverse' angles that the actions made in the previous Set-Ups are replicated correctly. The gun in Jack's hand, for example, needs to be in the same hand for the 'reverse' shots.

Now and again, keeping to the simple strictures of 'forward', 'one-directional' Shot Listing is not going to work for you. That occurs when a sequence is extremely detailed and complex and where shooting all the action in one direction and then returning to the start point to film the 'reverse' is going to make the sequence edit poorly or seem disjointed and jarring.

Take a look at some of the fight sequences in Quentin Tarantino's *Kill Bill* movies. They're complex and lengthy, yet they flow incredibly smoothly and believably. How did Tarantino achieve that? How did the technicians manage to shoot everything in one direction and yet come back to seamlessly film the reverse? How did the actors and stunt performers memorize so completely the moves they made over such extended time frames?

The answer is that Mr. Tarantino utilized the concept of K.I.S.S. He broke the fight scenes into bite-sized pieces. He'd shoot perhaps 3 to 5 'moves' — a thrust, a block, a counter-jab, a step aside, a turn — all from one direction, and then he'd immediately shoot the reverse. Yes, it might have taken time to re-set lighting (but perhaps not too much time if the plan had been carefully considered in pre-production) — but the actors would find it much easier to replicate those 3 to 5 moves in the reverse as the action and the physical space they moved in would be fresh in their minds. The same principle of recent muscle memory would help the technicians too, allowing the shots to match so much better in the edit. Further benefits? Using the 'bite-sized' progress through the sequence would have made continuity simpler — especially as, per the script, actors would progressively become bloodier or have clothing ripped and weapons damaged or broken.

But the Tarantino methodology wouldn't just assist the Costume and MUAH departments. Think about the Art Dept.! The trail of destruction would have evolved organically — no need to reset all the broken tables, chairs, props etc., with 'new' items and then hope that in the 'reverses' all the same items would break or be damaged in the same way as in the earlier shots.

So, something to bear in mind; when you start to feel over-whelmed and think that things are getting too complicated — take a deep breath. Then look for the simplest way to achieve what you are after.

All artforms have moments that appear to be hugely diffi-cult, but when they're broken down you will often find those moments can be captured in a manner so simple it will aston-ish you.

CHAPTER EIGHT

Edit Decision List

In some respects, your Shot List is also an Edit Decision List, because you should be making shots that are designed to be edited together. You'll have guessed by now that I am going to discuss editing in depth in *Cutting For Keeps* — yet another fine title in *The Filmmaker's Art* series. However, certain important 'editorial' concepts need to be grasped here in the final stages of the Pre-Production phase of your film.

Your job is to bring footage into the edit that can be edited. That sounds so simple that many filmmakers have taken it to mean that it doesn't really matter *what* you bring into the edit room, because the editor can sort it out. Taken to its logical conclusion, there are filmmakers who figure that if they give the editor a ton of footage, yards and yards of the stuff, then they will have given the grateful edit team 'coverage' and plenty of it. So what else could the Editor possibly want?

How about some decisions that you have already made so that hard drives are not filled with footage that will never be used, and assistant editors don't have their young lives wasted wading through hours and hours of material to find the few minutes of useable media that can be organized into the folders that the Editor will work with?

Reducing the amount of *'Give-Monkeys-Cameras-And-They'll-Eventually-Remake-Citizen-Kane'* footage is one thing. An awareness of issues that will elevate your Shot Listing and produce stronger material would be even better. I have three primary concepts to introduce which, if factored into the pre-production phase, might increase the likelihood of decent footage landing on the editorial hard drives. Here's a quick sketch of each so that you can begin to think about, and perhaps apply, the principles. They are;

- The Kuleshov Effect
- Intensified Continuity
- Average Shot Length

The Kuleshov Effect is one of the foundational principles of Editing. It was a phenomenon first demonstrated by Russian filmmaker Lev Kuleshov. In brief, it is the juxtaposition of shots within an edited sequence that produces a thought-process in the audience as to the emotion or attitude of an actor. You can find examples of it on the web, and Alfred Hitchcock actually filmed his own version — starring himself, of course — which is on You Tube. The Kuleshov Effect is in three parts. In the first shot, we see an actor looking at someone or something. In the second shot, we see the someone, or something, that the actor is looking at. In the third shot, we cut back to the first shot. In Kuleshov's experimental version, the actor's expression never changes. In Hitchcock's, the Great Man smiles in the final (third) shot. The sequence is then repeated, with an important difference. The shots of the actor (and of Hitchcock) remain *exactly* the same — but the shot that goes between (the second shot) is changed. In the Hitchcock version, the middle image is, first, a mother and child and, second, a lady in a revealing swimsuit. The audience thought-process seeing Hitchcock gazing at mother and child, then smiling, produces the reaction *'what a nice old man, look how charmed he is to see a blissful, innocent moment'*. The sequence which features Hitch regarding the blonde in the swimsuit produces quite a different audience thought-process and reaction. Especially in our more sensitive times. The shots of Mr. Hitchcock and the order in

which they were edited were *exactly the same*, but one sequence reveals him as a kindly, avuncular gent and the other
as a lecherous voyeur. You might now ask;

- *What does the 'Kuleshov Effect' reveal in terms of my
  Shot List and the footage I will bring to the Edit?*

A good question. All the tricks of filmmaking, we must remember, are essentially used in support of a lie. Cinema is a
form of magic. Just as the stage conjurer performs maneuvers
that trick us into believing one thing when the truth is another
thing entirely — filmmakers use techniques, the smoke and the
mirrors, to trick the audience into thinking and believing that
what they are watching is true. The Kuleshov Effect is a powerful weapon in the arsenal of such tricks because it makes the
audience come to a conclusion, or have a feeling, or experience an emotion. As every con artist knows, when the audience does the work, the 'belief' grows stronger.

In purely physical terms, juxtaposing two separate shots
does one of two things. It either unites or separates. Let me explain that paradox. In the Hitchcock example, because the
shots of the Great Man are connected to another shot — we
immediately believe that Hitch and the subjects of his observa-
tion are in the same place and time. But this is only because of
cinematic editing. Hitchcock's shot could have been taken outside his studio bungalow in winter, and the other shots could
have been made six months later in Pittsburgh. We were
shown a sequence that we believed to be true but in reality, it
was a lie. That's how film works. Robert Rodriquez and Frank
Miller film a crowded bar scene in *Sin City* (2005) — but in reality, none of the actors were present in Kadie's Bar at the same
time. And Kadie's Bar wasn't a bar. It was a stage set on a digital backlot, much of it being Green Screen. And although the
scene was filmed in color, the audience saw it in black & white
(with the exception of certain objects that were in color). I could
go on, but you get the idea. Lies, all of it! But I promise you, if
you can master this form of cinematic mendacity, using what

the Kuleshov Effect offers, you can become incredibly flexible in your staging, your blocking, your shooting, your direction.

What about the other side of the paradox? How does the Kuleshov Effect 'separate'? Answer; by making the audience think that the shots they are seeing are unified in Time and Space, and then revealing, in the manner of the stage magician, that this is not so — which produces its own reaction from the audience.

But as the original Kuleshov experiment — and Hitchcock's later demonstration of the Effect — proves, the most important aspect of the technique is how a juxtaposition of shots affects the mind of the audience and provokes a reaction or an inner and personal interpretation. I'll be returning to this in a later book in the series — *Actors On Set* — when I will discuss in depth how you can use the Effect with your thespians by asking them to have no reaction at all, or perhaps a very specific reaction, and then inserting the shot that will force the audience to use their own thought-process to work out what the character is thinking and feeling. Lev Kuleshov's insight gave filmmakers an incredible tool to draw out performance.

Consider. Every single Clint Eastwood movie you ever saw uses the Kuleshov Effect, relying on that actor's remarkable stillness to make the audience 'work'. In its purest Kuleshovian form, Mr. Eastwood doesn't have to react at all, and the audience knows *exactly* what he's thinking.

That's the quick overview. How can we apply it to the scenes we've been laboring over and introduce the technique into the Shot List?

Pierce comes out of the Abandoned Factory in Sc. 89 and cries '*Where is he?*' Let's say you have that line in MCU. The Kuleshov Effect triggers you to go to another shot — the empty roadway, the intact fence, the crickets chirping in the grass — and then return to Pierce in the MCU. You will have forced an emotional reaction — not from Pierce, but from the audience. Some will be thinking '*Hah, Pierce, you're screwed now, buddy!*' Others will be thinking '*Oh no! What's going to happen if nobody comes to the rescue?*' Still others might think, '*Easy, dude, Jack's on the way*'. A few might be thinking something entirely different and their focus is perhaps, '*Pierce is useless. Helen won't make it, it's over for her*' or '*If Helen hadn't put her trust in Jack this would never had happened in the first place!*' See what you've done? You've engaged the audience.

With an awareness of how the Kuleshov Effect will work in the Edit, you can now incorporate it, at your discretion, into your Shot List. The result? You will have made your audience have their own thoughts about what they are watching. Made them do half the work — which will strengthen the suspension of their disbelief in the 'lie' inherent in cinema. Made them involved in your story. They will love you for it.

Let's talk Intensified Continuity and Average Shot Length. Again, this is going to be discussed more fully in a future series title but here's the thumbnail.

Film academics, historians, and filmmakers take 'Intensified Continuity' to mean a contemporary style of film editing that relies upon multiple shots, edited in such a way that the 'average' shot length throughout a film tends to be measured in seconds rather than minutes. If a film runs for 2 hours — 7,200 seconds — and there are 1,400 cuts in that film, then the Average Shot Length (the edit itself, not the amount of footage acquired in a single take) would be 5.14 seconds, while the same total running time for a film with 650 cuts, would increase the ASL to 11.07 seconds.

There's a great deal of argument and discussion surrounding the issue, with academics like David Bordwell and Kristin Thompson at the forefront of a fascinating subject. One of the best ways to glimpse the workings of Intensified Continuity, Mr. Bordwell suggests, is to compare remakes with their originals and notice how the number of shots used to convey a scene in a contemporary remake of a movie compares to the earlier original version of the same scene. But while 'Intensified Continuity' seems to be an *editorial* technique, it cannot be applied if the principle has not been allowed for in a pre-production Shot List. To my mind, 'Intensified Continuity' is a *production* technique because the shots are manipulated and controlled in Production, long before they arrive in the Edit.

People tend to forget how slowly film used to move. The shots were lengthy, the cuts slow and deliberate. Part of the reason was that filmmakers understood, especially in the early years, that the medium was new. Some people 'got' it quickly and understood the 'language' the filmmakers were speaking. Others found it difficult to understand. Sometimes, even the simple connection between two shots — an exterior of a train leaving a station, followed by an interior shot of a character in the club car — would be confusing to some viewers. I'm old enough to remember elderly people for whom television was a completely new experience and who didn't understand story-lines because the characters kept popping up in different places, or characters they didn't recognize would suddenly appear out of nowhere.

Around 50 years ago, filmmakers started to consciously speed up the language, assuming that if they did so the audiences would become more fluent. To some extent, this worked — but there was a resistance in the mainstream because producers and exhibitors realized that there was still a substantial audience that didn't take kindly to new-fangled methods and filmmakers 'speaking' too quickly to be understood.

Skip forward to the men and women who changed that. The 1980s music video directors. Amongst whom I am numbered. I am aware that many will dispute the idea that music video changed the way audiences understand and watch film. But I was present and can bear witness. In fact, I was so conflicted about 'Intensified Continuity' that several of the music videos I co-directed — like Bob Dylan's *Emotionally Yours*, or

Eurythmics' *There Must Be An Angel (Playing With My Heart)*, were deliberate refutations of the technique and were shot and edited in ways that far exceeded the conventional Average Shot Length associated with MTV.

So, I say it again. I say it loud and I say it proud. The music video directors of the early-MTV era changed the film and television industries forever by familiarizing worldwide audiences with 'Intensified Continuity' — a fast-paced, rapid-cut editorial technique coupled with a production aesthetic that completely disregarded traditional framing and camera movement. Of course, we didn't invent it. We'd spent our young lives in seedy art-house theaters breathlessly watching films made with hand-held 16mm cameras by artists like Jean-Luc Godard.

Things were done in 80s music video that dismissed the rules of previous generations. Hefty 35mm cinema cameras like the Arriflex BL3 were attached to ropes and swung at the talent because a crane wasn't going to make the shot the way the director wanted. Perfect framing was rejected for angles and frames that were wildly 'incorrect' by conventional standards. Cheaply emotive storylines were told, in full, in under three minutes. Directors and producers kept pushing manufacturers for equipment that would make a shot so unusual it would be the talk of the water-cooler for a week or elevate an entire production company into 'flavor of the month'. Production designers, costumers and lighting departments were given huge scope to intensify the elements present in the frame, an amplification consciously chosen to grab interest and attention. The way in which shots were made, and the way those shots were edited — with drastic reductions in the length of time a shot was allowed to be onscreen (some music videos had 400 edit events in 3 minutes) — barely gave the average viewer time to understand what they were seeing. Music video was so intense that its 'language' became a 'jargon' that only a younger demographic understood.

But that demographic was important to advertisers, so music video production and editorial techniques started showing up on television. The faster editing. The jerky, hand-held shots. The reduction of Average Shot Length. Music video directors found themselves directing episodes of cutting-edge shows like *Miami Vice*. Important and established filmmakers started either making music videos themselves (and, boy, some of them didn't have a clue what they were doing) or incorporated music video techniques into television dramas and high-end commercials.

And once that happened, after lengthy arguments, it slowly began to happen in feature films. The central topic of discussion (which took place, I realize, in the years before many of my readers were born), was that fast cuts and obtrusive camera motion could not, and would not, translate to the big screen. There was a consensus for a time that the techniques of music video would cause motion sickness and epileptic fits in cinema audiences. Those music video directors who got the chance to make their debut features (like myself) hesitated. Almost without exception, we made our debut films in 'traditional' ways and pulled back on our intensified continuity techniques. There was even a brief moment in the early-to-mid 90s when feature filmmakers wondered aloud if the ease and speed of editing a film on an Avid Media Composer would in itself cause Average Shot Length (ASL) to decrease and literally force normally staid and conservative editors into 'Intensified Continuity'. In 1996 Kathryn Bigelow made a film called *Strange Days*. I recall filmmakers of my acquaintance who argued that the 'Intensified Continuity' had produced a film that, when screened in theaters, was too fast and uncomfortable to watch. It's hard to believe, but it's true. More recently, there was debate that one of the *Jason Bourne* films had applied 'Intensified Continuity' a little too eagerly and harshly — and that some viewers found it hard to watch in theaters. So, you must ask yourself;

- *What will Intensified Continuity and the reduction of Average Shot Length mean for my Shot List?*

When I started out in the 80s, theatrical feature filmmakers could count on one page of script equaling one minute of edited screen-time. But audiences now accept information faster. Much faster. It's a fact of life that audiences all over the world know the language of film so well they can take in a page of script in 45 seconds or less. You and your editor better understand that, or your film will seem dull to a contemporary audience.

The current rate of ASL requires you to be aware that you can't linger on a shot forever and a day, unless there is a good reason to do so. In short, don't get lazy — keep shooting useable footage for as long as your schedule allows. Think about which scenes require intensity and movement, and which ones can be static and languid. Average Shot Length is an 'average' of all the shots in your film, not a requirement for each individual shot. In the Shot List we've been working with, Sc. 16 at the 'Abandoned Factory' might be 'Intense' with a series of quick-cut shots as JACK arrives and kicks open the door to the old building. Sc. 89 might be much slower, perhaps a traditional and lengthy 2-Shot as Pierce and Helen come out of the building — while Intensified Continuity could be reintroduced with an adrenalin rush for the truck/fence action of Sc. 91.

As for the herky-jerky intensity of camera movement — don't think that you are required to start flinging your camera around and requesting barrel rolls and back-flips — but do consider movement and find ways to keep your shots interesting. More importantly, make sure you get enough shots. The most excruciating moment in a Director's life comes when an Editor turns in her chair and asks, 'Do you have another shot?'

Try to have another shot. Especially if you're shooting 'micro' budget — because having those extra shots will elevate your production value.

During filming of *The Missing Link*, camera motion systems were not available to me. So, to get 'movement', and keep my

Average Shot Length at a contemporary 'rate' for a drama, I
kept repositioning the camera and getting a fresh angle of the
same action, or a specific moment in the action. That way, I
brought multiple shots into the edit for each scene and I could
cut around them, making the audience unaware of the limitations of camera movement I'd been faced with.

Finally, in this chapter, a word about Transitions. As you
consider each scene, you should be envisioning how it follows
on from the previous scene and how you are going to get out
of the scene you're working on once it's over. Bearing in mind
that scenes are usually part of longer sequences, it's incredibly
satisfying when a simple cut takes you from one 'scene' to another. In the example we've been using to build our Shot List,
the entrance of JACK in the BMW (Sc. 16) could have been a
cut from the interior of the BMW as Jack swung around the
corner and accelerated towards the Abandoned Factory. We'd
need to read Sc. 15 to know for sure. The conclusion of Sc. 92
has us holding on the truck as it disappears into the distance.
This invites many kinds of transition — from a simple cut into
the truck to continue with our trio, or to the bad guys bemoaning the fact that the good guys have got away. Equally, the
shot could fade to black and the following scene fade in with
Jack at another location; 'The Next Day'.

Directors and Editors ultimately collaborate on how to transition — but the edit is using footage that has already been
captured and 'directed', so the director must consider the
ways in and out of every scene and incorporate those into the
Shot List.

Sometimes, Screenwriters can't help themselves and indicate how a scene should end or begin.

FADE IN, CUT, SMASH CUT, HARD CUT, DISSOLVE,
WIPE, FADE TO BLACK.

Screenwriting software has drop-down menus to help writ-
ers add their transitions. It's as if the scribes believe

themselves to be directors or editors, the poor dears. All that additional work for no reason. You will, of course, ignore their instructions with the exception of FADE IN: at the very beginning of the screenplay and FADE TO BLACK: at the end.

Everything else is not a scribe's job.

CHAPTER NINE

Beyond Coverage

As you read the various titles already published, or yet to be published, in *The Filmmaker's Art* series, you may glimpse that I am a Hitchcock fan. Although I admire too many filmmakers to mention, Alfred Hitchcock was and remains my first love. When I was a small boy, I had a *Cinema Paradiso* experience and learnt how to project film. The first film I projected on my own was a 16mm print of *The 39 Steps*. The screening pretty much sealed my fate and my future. As I projected the film, I felt an over-whelming responsibility; to the film, to the audience and to Mr. Hitchcock. To be in the audience — and yet, not to be 'in the audience' but instead be the person responsible for the story continuing uninterrupted and as the filmmaker intended it to be (i.e. in focus) had a powerful effect on me. I understood in that moment how filmmakers have to be both audience and technician/artist. As *The 39 Steps* unspooled, I began to notice how the audience's attention and reaction shifted constantly with the unfolding story. It was a curious sensation to feel an awareness that I had (thanks to the film) a mastery over the audience that I didn't fully understand — but felt. My job was to operate and safeguard a machine that was throwing back into the *real* world the material which Mr. Hitchcock had captured from a *fantasy* world, via a similar magical machine. I was the 'Projectionist', while Mr. Hitchcock had been, for want of a better word, the 'Ingestionist'. We were at opposite ends of the same production pipeline. He'd put the images 'in' and I was responsible for putting them 'out' in the way he'd intended. We were kindred spirits, occupying a special space; 'in' the audience, but not 'of' the audience. I had a childlike epiphany that, because I had been given charge of *The 39 Steps*, I stood by that Projector on Mr. Hitchcock's behalf, *in loco parentis*. Clearly, at 10 years old, I was an overly-serious and possibly a slightly mad child. I couldn't have put that epiphany into words at the time. Even today, I still find it difficult to describe how pivotal the moment was in my life and how strange and exhilarating it was to be completely engaged in the film yet have a simultaneous ability to detach myself and observe the audience — all the while remaining keenly aware of 'quality control' and the technical requirements to successfully project the film.

I studied Hitchcock's films avidly for years. When I co-directed my first feature *Murder Story* (1989) I had a copy of *Truffaut/Hitchcock* on the nightstand in my hotel room. A talisman to refer to if I lost confidence or got into trouble. One of the most interesting things about Hitchcock is his relationship with the Editorial Department and how he would shoot for the edit. The work we've being doing in *Shooting The List* has mostly been figuring out how to efficiently and creatively bring footage into the edit — a process Hitchcock was a master of (as was his wife and collaborator, Alma Reville).

I hope that in reading this book you've seen that using the discipline of working through a scene to create a Shot List doesn't just give you the security of working out your 'coverage'. It distills your 'vision' by forcing you to think how to transfer an image or concept from your imagination, first onto paper and then, through a hard and demanding physical process, onto your production hard drives. Production is essentially an intermediate process between script and edit. A process that Hitchcock described as 'working in the coalmine'. For Hitchcock, the detail of his planning often meant that the production itself was tedious. Rather like wading through a hefty book for the second time, the project had already become too familiar. It might even have felt to the Maestro that when he shot the film he'd so carefully planned… he was making it for the second time.

I started this book by identifying 'coverage' as the first and most important aspect of your Shot List build. Other bene-fits arose. The ability to identify structural or temporal flaws in the screenplay. The necessity of having the geography of phys-ical spaces, and how your actors move in those spaces, clearly mapped out in your mind. The time-saving and contingency-providing decisions that allow you to overcome budget and scheduling limitations. The refinements you can make to give scenes more impact. The efficiencies of deciding, in the calm of pre-production, what choices will work best in terms of lens, camera, movement, equipment and blocking. The ability to make notes and reminders to yourself so that you don't slip up when time is pressing, and your attention is pulled in multiple directions.

That said, although Building a Shot List is work — and often laborious work —it's a simple enough process in itself.

However, in my Hitchcockian studies, I came across a methodology in Sir Alfred's art that can best be described as 'Beyond Coverage', or even 'Anti-Coverage' — and as soon as I understood it, I began to see how other filmmakers apply the same deliberate and conscious abandonment of 'coverage' — although not always for the same reasons.

I seem to have suggested that getting 'coverage' is the single most important task you undertake as a director in pre-production. I've done this deliberately — because I wanted you to start thinking about your edit and the footage you would take into your edit. Further, when you shoot for 'coverage' you are less likely to make mistakes and find yourself blamed for missing something obvious and important. Nobody ever got fired for shooting 'coverage'.

But now I'm going to suggest the opposite. I am about to urge you to not to shoot 'coverage'. Anarchy or Art? Confusion or Cunning? I'll let you decide.

When I learned that my hero, Alfred Hitchcock, would on occasion deliberately not shoot 'coverage', I became intrigued. The reasoning — which you would think unnecessary given his eminence and the majority of his budgets — was to protect his 'vision' and his artistry. By consciously shooting specific shots, and *only* those specific shots, he was able to control what was edited — even if studio executives (and, by implication, potential future owners of the material) sought to change or exert control over his work. In short, the footage he shot was so precisely garnered that there was only a small number of ways to edit it together. Ultimately, the result Hitchcock wanted was this; that there would be only one way to assemble the shots that would make any sense.

The Hitchcock Way.

It seems reckless to risk not getting the shots you need in the hope of only getting the shots you will use. Doesn't it? Surely, 'protecting' your so-called 'vision' is only worthwhile if you have a 'vision' worth protecting, otherwise it's merely arrogance. It seems reasonable for the likes of Alfred Hitchcock or Orson Welles to take such an approach — but lesser luminaries? Well, it turns out that those of us who aspire to improve our filmmaking and perhaps have our work bear a fuller artistic signature might take a moment to examine the concept of 'Anti-Coverage' and go One Step Beyond.

I'm not a fan of David Mamet's work either on stage or on film. I am, however, a fan of Mr. Mamet's intellect. And I find much to admire in his book *On Directing Film* (Penguin, 1992). At the time of writing, Mamet was clearly influenced by Kuleshov and the pure cinema derived from a careful selection and juxtaposition of shots. He urged that each scene should be considered for its meaning — and once that 'meaning' had been distilled to its essence, then a decision could be arrived at with regard to the shot(s). By working in this way, Mamet suggested, the end result would always be 'Art' — because the artist had processed how 'Meaning' could be derived from the scene.

Granted, that's all well and good. However, to remain employable in the world's film industries and not be written off as an obscurist or, worse, as pretentious — care has to be taken when investing your scene with 'Meaning' through Kuleshovian juxtaposition.

You will recall that in the chapter 'Building The List', I arrived at a neat bundle of Shots for Scs. 16, 89 and 91.

My purpose was to familiarize you with the basics of 'coverage' and give you a glimpse into how to create tone and build on theme with maximum speed and efficiency. The Shot List did what it was required to do — which was to show the circumstances our three characters found themselves in and the actions they took. Urgency and Action were explicit in the shots.

The way the Shot List was constructed, however, was to maximize 'coverage' so that final decisions could be arrived at later in the edit. It was primarily a 'safe' Shot List. Everything the producer or an editor would need was there.

It was not, however, a particularly *artistic* Shot List. Oh, the building blocks were present and from those elements something 'artistic' could certainly be created. There would be enough, and the edit would prove that the footage was 'well-directed'. But because the Shot List was primarily about 'Coverage' it was missing a crucial element.

Focus.

In Chapter 4, I suggested that the first question to ask your-self prior to building your Shot List was; '*What needs to be ac-complished?*' I mentioned in passing that this, in fact, was not the question you ought to have asked. But we followed the 'wrong' question to its conclusion anyway, and— with some satisfying results — built a Shot List with 'coverage'. However, to be better-than-average filmmakers, we need to go 'Beyond Coverage'. We need to take a step back when we begin to build our Shot List and instead of asking '*What do I need?*' we should ask;

- *What is the meaning of this scene, and why is it in the script?*

In the lesson David Mamet offers us, by way of Lev Kule-shov, the question boils down to this;

- *What is this scene about?*

So, let's go back to the Abandoned Factory and ask;

- *What's it all about, Alfie?*

First and foremost, it's about Urgency. All three scenes carry a Time Factor and a sense that it may already be too late.

Sc. 16 has the idea of one man trying to restore order or find solutions. It's dawn. JACK's the only person on the street. So, it's also about one man's solitary, even lonely, ac-tion. The gun means the possibility of violent action. Can we go 'beyond coverage' and get the meaning of scene over to the audience in a clear and uncompromising series of juxtaposed shots? Can we create, for this one small scene, a cinematic ex-perience that goes beyond the easy and the trite?

Sc. 89 ramps up the Urgency. PIERCE, frantic and anx-ious, yelling '*where is he?*' HELEN, beaten almost into uncon-sciousness. The evidence of Violence writ large. Can we go 'beyond coverage' and put that meaning across so vividly the audience mimic Pierce's anxieties in their own bodies, clenching their fists, tightening their collective stomachs, feeling outrage and empathy at Helen's condition?

Sc. 91. The catharsis to Sc. 89's anxiety. The truck arrives — crashing through the fence and coming to the rescue. A relief immediately replaced by a different tension and anxiety — can they get away in time? Urgency reasserts itself. The Violence has been transferred to the truck. Jack's 'violence' is no longer confined to carrying a gun and kicking open a door. Now he uses a truck to barrel through a fence — not once, but twice!

Using a variation on a principle that Francis Coppola advocates, I've chosen three words to tell me what these scenes are about. *Urgency. Isolation. Violence.* (a) The *Urgency* of the Situation, and the sense that there is a ticking clock. (b) The *Isolation* of Jack, a protagonist acting on his own for the benefit of others. (c) The sense of imminent, and present, *Violence*.

If I can get those three *meaningful* conceptual ideas across to the audience then I think I will hold their interest in the story and get them to ask themselves, '*What's going to happen next?*' I will attempt to go 'Beyond Coverage' to get pure cinema shots. As I work through Sc. 16, I'm going to place the shots in editorial order (not in shooting order) so that you can visualize the scene as it will be projected. Using the three concepts that will give 'meaning', here's my first pass.

Isolation. I'm going to introduce Sc. 16 with a sense of emptiness which, when JACK's BMW appears, will make it seem like Jack is alone in a big space — one man against the world. That shot will be LONG and HI-ANGLE, looking towards the deserted early-morning street corner where the car will appear. I will *hear* Jack's car before I see it, perhaps for many long seconds — so the shot will stay on an unmoving streetscape until a loud-engined car appears, moving recklessly fast, in a place of silence and emptiness.

Urgency. I will cut to the fast-moving TRACKING shot along the length of the fence, as JACK's BMW screeches to a halt. I am still enamored of the idea that Jack is always coming up against barriers. It's one of my Image Systems for this movie.

Urgency. I will cut to a LO-ANGLE CLOSE-UP of the left front tire/fender of the car as it brakes and stops.

Urgency. I will fast TRUCK in a LO-ANGLE MEDIUM to MEDIUM CLOSE-UP as Jack steps out of the car. In the same shot I will add — Violence — using a TILT down to see the GUN in Jack's hands for a brief moment (he will rack a round into the chamber) before his lower body leaves frame.

Isolation. I will cut back to the HI-ANGLE, LONG shot again, watching as JACK runs towards the abandoned building. The car with its open door will be in the lower foreground (f.g). This is a continuation of the first shot in the sequence.

Violence. A REVERSE TRUCK in MEDIUM shot that moves parallel, and just ahead of, JACK as he runs towards the door, and PANS L-R to capture the final moment as he kicks the door open and leaves frame.

Isolation. A final cut back to the HI-ANGLE, LONG shot as JACK, having kicked open the door, disappears inside the building. The shot will hold on the scene for at least 4 seconds.

To save time (by keeping the camera moving forward from the first to last positions) I'd shoot the sequence out of the order that the shots would eventually be edited in. Like this;

LS, HI-ANG, PAN R-L — entire action
CU, LO-ANG, BABY LEGS — car in
MS/MCU, LO-ANGLE, TILT — Jack out, w/gun

FS/WS, TRACK, L-R — fence in f.g., car in, Jack out, runs…
REV TRUCK, MS, PAN L-R — Jack runs, door kick

That's a Shot List made by an accommodating, reasonable director who doesn't want to scare a producer unnecessarily. But, on the day, only two shots really count, a third is a luxury and two are clichés which are only there to help if I need a more intensified continuity.

The two vital shots are the HI-ANGLE LONG shot which begins and ends the scene, and the MEDIUM to MEDIUM CLOSE-UP of the gun being racked as Jack gets out of the car. With those two shots, I think I can convey Isolation, Urgency and Violence. I will have gone 'Beyond Coverage' because there will be only one way to cut the scene. No further choices will be available.

The luxury shot is the TRACK along the fence. I love my baby. Which means I must kill it.

The first cliché shot is the big CLOSE UP on the tire as the BMW slews to a stop. The second is a less clichéd shot, but a cliché nonetheless — the REVERSE TRUCK for the running door kick. Both must go.

So, if we are to go 'Beyond Coverage' and enter a world where the film can only be cut one way — the way that you have designed it in your Shot List — we are left with two Set-Ups. Shot #1 being the Hi-Angle Long Shot and Shot #2 the Medium/Medium Close Up of Jack and, more importantly, his weapon.

The important factor to remember is that all the Shots you make must have a purpose and contain 'Meaning'.

Shot #1: My LS/HI-ANG shot is not neutral. It is of a scene waiting for something to happen. It implies Isolation. The empty street, the sound of the approaching car, the solitariness of the car when it appears, and its speed (contrasted with the stillness of the street). The tension emphasized by slightly erratic driving and good sound effects. All of that conveys both Isolation and Urgency. Further conveyed when we see Jack quickly exit the car and hurry towards the building. Holding on Shot #1 once Jack has kicked the door open and gone inside increases the tension and reinforces both Isolation and the sense of impending Violence. We don't know, in our example, what is going to happen in Sc. 17 when Jack is inside the building but staying on the shot at the end of Sc. 16, once Jack's disappeared from view, forces the audience into the desired thought pattern — 'what's going to happen next?'. You haven't told them yet, so they're prepared to sit and wait for the story to unfold because you've made them interested in this fast-driving guy with a gun.

Shot #2: The MS/MCU, LO-ANG, with TILT to the gun says Violence, with a side dish of Urgency. And, of course, we remember another Hitchcockian maxim, via Anton Chekov — that once a gun is shown in a drama, it is necessary for that gun to be used.

By inserting Shot #2 (the MS/MCU) between the two parts of Shot #1 (the HI-ANG/LS), a perfect Kuleshovian triptych has been formed — showing an Isolated environment, and a Violent protagonist Urgently hurrying towards whatever happens next.

Having read Sc. 89 again for its 'meaning' I realize that I can repeat the three motivators — Urgency, Violence and Isolation — that were my touchstones for Sc. 16. Could I make a similar Kuleshovian Triptych for Sc. 89 as I had for Sc. 16?

Bien sûr, mes amis.

The first and last shots in the Triptych would be a shot that starts *'out of focus'* in FS as PIERCE and HELEN stagger towards camera and the intermediate shot would be a POV.

FS to MS. No FOCUS PULL Pierce & Helen move into focus
HH/WS/POV — mimicking Pierce's view of fence/empty road

Why would I start Sc. 89 'out of focus', only allowing
Helen and Pierce to 'sharpen' gradually — probably mid-way
between their start point and the MS of their final position?
First, it increases Isolation — two indistinct and blurred
figures, their outlines distorted. The subjects are distanced
from the observer. Second, it adds tension. If the audience
doesn't know exactly what they're seeing, other than the
shapes of the two figures approaching (staggering, one sup-
porting the other), then they're going to wonder what happened, or is going to happen. The slow reveal as to the extent
of Helen's injuries as she comes into focus allows the viewer to
fully take in the Violence that has occurred. Thirdly, I might be
playing with an Image System where, throughout the film, it
takes a moment before things get fully revealed or become
clear (and coming up with an idea like that while building a
Shot List is yet another 'positive' reason for doing the work).
Lastly, and perhaps this is reaching a little for something that
might not be there — but which, after all, is what artists do),
being 'out of focus' and gradually coming 'into focus' could
subliminally be suggesting Helen's state of consciousness,
given that she's been badly beaten.

The middle shot of the Triptych, (Pierce's POV) is a
loose Hand-Held shot which mimics the kinetic energy of
Pierce's frantic search for signs of Jack's arrival. By scanning
the empty street, we're increasing 'Isolation' and adding a
soupçon of 'Urgency' that Pierce's dialogue and expressions
will amplify.

You'll have noticed that I have abandoned the earlier
REVERSE in Sc. 89 to get Pierce and Helen to a position where
I can leave them while we insert Sc. 90. Why? Because, in Pre-
Production I made the decision to delete Sc. 90 and keep the
audience firmly in place. No, I'm not cheating — I'm directing!

How are we doing for Time? Due to the HI-ANGLE for shot #1 (which might require a crane) and the nature of working with a car, Sc 16 should take 30 to 45 minutes to shoot. Sc. 89 now has two shots. 20 minutes — 30 at the outside. That will leave at least 1.5 hours to film Sc. 91, for breakfast at 8.30 a.m., or a full 2 hours if those caterers show up late.

Sc. 91 has to blast us out of our seats. It needs multiple shots to achieve Intensified Continuity, an intensity increased by keeping our Shot Length tight. Although much of the Intensified Continuity will happen in the Edit with sharp cutting, we still need to bring enough Shots into post-production.

- *It's easy to understand how using Intensified Continuity in Sc. 91 will contribute to Urgency and Violence. But how will Isolation be maintained?*

It doesn't have to be maintained. The motivators of Urgency, Violence and Isolation are not required to be our touchstones for the entire film. These are not Thematic Assistants, Phrases or Statements that keep us in touch with the bones of the complete story (to fully understand this terminology, see *Decoding The Script*). They are words that allow us to distill the meaning of a specific scene. It so happens that the words that worked to give meaning to Sc. 16 worked equally well with Sc. 89. At least two of the words — Urgency and Violence — could be applicable for Sc. 91 and that might be enough. Given that every filmmaker has a unique interpretation of a script, and may derive different meanings from a scene, we could leave it at Urgency and Violence. Equally, we could add 'Joy' and get that across in the performances and in swooping camera movements. We could substitute 'Fear'. Or retain Isolation. That would be my choice, because I like the Shot on the track that holds the trio in LS as they stumble to get into the truck. Small figures in a threatening world. Isolated. I also like the idea that all the exterior scenes shot at the 'Abandoned Factory' location should reinforce, however subliminally, those three 'Meanings'. So, I'd keep the Sc.91 Shot List as it stands — there's more than enough material there to encapsulate the three 'Meanings' with Intensified Continuity.

- *Then what happens to your Kuleshov Effect, Mr. Innocenti? Do you conveniently forget about it now that Intensified Continuity is the goal?*

Of course not. In our edit, we use the Effect even more dramatically than we did in Scs. 16 and 89. We break our Sc. 91 sequence with its multiple shots into Kuleshovian pieces. The difference is that instead of Sc. 91 having a single Kuleshov Effect — it has several, all happening with dramatically decreased Shot Length.

For example; (i) the truck blasts through the fence, (ii) Pierce reacts (iii) the truck keeps ploughing onwards.

Next time you watch an action sequence, notice how Kuleshov triptychs are dropped in. The standard one is that powerful moment when the two heroes, on the verge of committing themselves to a high-risk maneuver, (i) first look at each other, (ii) look at whatever it is they must confront, and then (iii) exchange a final look before launching themselves into the fray. This Kuleshov triptych allows us to: (i) See our heroes realize that it's do-or-die time and they must risk everything. (ii) Their POV, the middle of the trio of shots, reminds us of the terrible danger and (iii) The last 'exchange of looks' (which with the majority of star actors is almost exactly the same expression as the first) puts the thought into the audience's mind that these guys are absolutely heroic and completely wonderful, despite the overwhelming odds against success.

If you stay Kuleshovian in your edit, using bite-size pieces of your footage — you'll end up with Intensified Continuity, low ASL, Cinematic Purity (Kuleshov) and 'Meaning'. We'll discuss this more fully when Vol. 6 in the series comes around.

For now, let's move on.

CHAPTER TEN

Production Moments

As I think has been fully demonstrated, there's a multitude of ways to shoot a scene. Even in our small, 3-scene single-page example we've worked through a variety of Lists, all of which will produce a result. At the end of the day, how you approach a Shot List is a matter of synthesizing in your own head all the factors that are going to either limit your options or point to solutions. Having worked through our examples you now have the knowledge, insight and understanding to balance the technical, the logistical and the creative. Where that balance lies, the weight given to each, will be your choice. Your judgment. When you implement those choices, extrapolated through hundreds of Set-ups, your unique signature will appear — good, bad or indifferent. The artistry and artisanship of your storytelling, its freshness or its lack, will be clearly revealed.

I've made a case for Shot Listing and for thoughtful preparation in Pre-Production. You can be as rigid with your List as you like, but you must also accept that the unexpected is a frequent visitor to your sets — a visitor who must be confronted and dealt with. Back in Chapter 4 (page 55) I mentioned that there was a 'hidden element' that I would leave to later. It's a small point, but something every 'technical' person finds themselves facing sooner or later.

Humans. Or, in our case — Actors.

Sc. 16 had a fast, and precise, 'drive-in' with a BMW. Your Shot List will have to be modified if the Actor playing JACK can't drive, or if the Production Insurance prohibits it. After all, the 'drive-in' is, technically, a STUNT. If the Precision Driver brings the BMW in, then additional or modified shots will be needed to get JACK out of the car, and also to disguise the fact that JACK is not at the wheel when the car arrives. Those are small technical adjustments, easily made. But, for a Director dealing with an Actor, there may well be an unexpected 'issue'. An Actor who insists on doing his own 'drive-in', or who feels slighted that he is not trusted to do it himself. An issue that, in pre-production, never occurred to you can suddenly cause a problem on your set — and, in this business, a problem can soon turn into a crisis.

Shooting The List is not the place to go into how Directors deal with the human elements of directing Actors. That's a discussion for *Actors On Set*. For now, in Pre-Production, keep in mind that when you build your Shot List your choices need a measure of flexibility to compensate for any issues that the human element will bring.

There isn't much anecdotal evidence of how the great filmmakers prepare what they are going to shoot — or how they implement those plans. But here's one, told to me by someone who worked with Stanley Kubrick on *Full Metal Jacket* (1987), describing how every day started. The location? An island in the middle of the Thames River in the heart of London. An obvious place, you will agree, to stage the Vietnam War's Tet Offensive. The time? Early morning. Cue action.

Mr. Kubrick would exit his trailer, gather his Department Heads around him and walk the exterior location. Every so often, he'd stop, survey the vista in front of him, then spit on the ground and issue a curt instruction — such as;

'50mm, 4 feet'.

With that, he'd move on. Camera Assistants would dutifully mark the spot where Stanley's Spittle lay, while Assistant Directors, Key Grips and Script Supervisor would make a careful note of his comment (50mm being the required lens and 4' being the camera height). Mr. Kubrick would proceed from point to point across the location, mapping out the entire day's shooting with spit and brief commands. No doubt his mouth was so dry after all that spitting, he was ready for the first cup of coffee. During the day, as each Set-up was reached, the camera would be placed directly on the 'spit mark' and given the lens requested and the camera height indicated. Looking through the camera would invariably produce *exactly* the framing that Kubrick required.

It helps when you have the brain of a Chess Grand Master.

In concluding this penultimate chapter, I should point out that there comes a time when you'll be directing film without a Shot List. You might imagine that the last thing you want is to be trying to make up your mind about the next shot when you're standing alone in the full glare of a busy set, but even that has an enjoyment to it if you're confident enough — like a tightrope walker daring himself to perform without a safety net for an audience thrilled by the audacity.

When I started in the business – as a young director – I had a Producer who realized how scared and unsure I was. He took me aside and said, *'In a few months, everything you're doing will seem easy. It'll just be like any 9-5 job. You won't be worried about it, you won't even think about it. You'll just do it.'*

It's true. It becomes second nature after a while – but I've always felt the danger of that was keeping things fresh and not just doing the same thing over and over again. So, before any project, I spend time absorbing the mental images that my reading of the script evokes. These I take into a Shot List.

But… my filmmaking nowadays often involves having no time, no budget and no resources. So, when I talk of directing without a Shot List, I don't mean because you no longer need one — but that a Shot List is impossible because you arrive on a set or a location without the luxury of adequate pre-production planning, or with the knowledge that everything you have planned will have to be changed.

For that reason, I know I must be able to visualize a whole scene so well, and know the material I need so thoroughly, that any upset from the planned scenario can be dealt with. Take, for example, a situation where you arrive at the location to find that (i) due to budget reasons there has been no Film Permit issued, (ii) one of your five actors has gotten lost on the way and is now somewhere near the Arizona border, (iii) your 1st Assistant Camera got a better paying gig, (iv) the Jib crane you wanted turned out to be too expensive but the U.P.M forgot to tell you, (v) the Costume Dept., have neglected to bring something vital, (vi) likewise the Art. Dept., and (vii) the PA wants to know if you'd prefer 1000 Island or Ranch Dressing with your lunchtime salad.

Take a deep breath. A Shot List that included 5 actors, a crane and some serious follow-focus work (courtesy of the 1st Assistant Camera) just went out the window. As did your all-day shoot — given that LAPD will probably close you down within an hour or two for not having that Permit. Allow yourself a moment to reflect on either (a) how pitiful your filmmaking career has become or (b) that these situations are but temporary obstacles on your journey to greater and more glorious things — and then face up to the challenge.

A 3-page scene? Okay — distribute the lines that should have been done by the 'lost' actor to the others. Rewrite if required. In fact, delete whole paragraphs if that helps. Eliminate the needed prop. Costume? If it can be fixed in 10 minutes — good. If not — forget about it. No crane? No focus-pulling? No need to quit! Move the actors, not the camera. Block out your scene. Watch carefully to see where the movement is and the moments you simply must have. Throw out all the ideas you previously had in your Shot List. It's no longer that movie. Start shooting. Maybe you do the entire scene Hand-Held on a wide-angle lens, aperture wide open so you and your Cinematographer don't need to worry about focus. Maybe you get some of the scene shot with the camera on top the Producer's SUV to get a little of that height your crane shot would have given you. As each shot is done, you've got to ask yourself; *'What else do I need to get to keep this scene tight and sharp in the edit room?'* The Cinematographer has a phrase for this that you'll hear often; *'What else do we owe*?' As in, *'what do we still need to shoot to have a full accounting of the scene – to have full coverage'*? You'll find your brain working overtime, doing what it's supposed to do — working out the edit in your mind and making sure you have those shots. Often, a remarkable thing will happen. An idea will be sparked. You'll ask the Cinematographer to set up a shot, and you may get a puzzled look because she's focused on 'got-to-have' material. Well, if you've already got what you have to have, always allow yourself the luxury of the shot that isn't absolutely necessary — because sometimes that's the shot in the final film that people will remember and talk about. And if you work fast, you'll be done just around the time the uniformed authorities arrive. Take the media out of the camera. Stick it in your pocket and casually walk back to your car. Let your Producer deal with the unsmiling Officers.

That's what's he's there for.

CHAPTER ELEVEN

Good. Fast. Cheap.

Filmmaking is an art that requires painstaking detailed work if it's going to elevate itself into something great. But, as I mentioned previously, I don't want you to think that every scene you ever shoot has to be pored over, analyzed and dissected in microscopic detail. Very often that is neither possible nor worthwhile. If you've managed to stay with me throughout this book, you have my thanks. I know Shot Listing is a tedious subject for discussion — but I also hope that you've had some insights that will help you get more efficiency and impact into your Principal Photography. Yes, there are scenes in every project that need careful examination — and the more you exercise your brain to come up with optimum solutions for tricky scenes, the faster and more effortless it becomes when you're presented with an easy scene. In fact, as your familiarity with how to proceed through a scene with economy and speed becomes second nature to you, the less you will need to have a Shot List. To use the music analogies I'm fond of, you will soon be able to shoot without 'looking at the sheet music' and even begin to improvise in ways that will impress your crew and please your audience. As we leave this book, and the final volume of my three-part examination of the Pre-Production Phase, here's a simple example for a 2-page dialogue scene.

We're back to that 'stoner' cult favorite *The Missing Link*. I say 'favorite' advisedly. The reviews were 'mixed' to say the least.

The following scene was an ensemble piece where the characters wonder how their leader ('Grog') is going to solve the problem of their runaway women. The edited scene lasts 2 minutes onscreen and uses a MASTER, several DIRTY SINGLES and a couple of shots that are CUTAWAYS — one of which, the group's POV of 'Grog', was shot elsewhere on a different day. There were 8 separate shots and it took less than an hour to shoot. The location was a small stream. Cinematographer David Lassiter placed the camera on BABY LEGS in the middle of the stream and we used a TILT from the stream to the group to make the MASTER and give a good TRANSITION from the previous scene. Two of characters either entered, or exited, the frame during the Master Shot.

MAS/WS, BABY LEGS, LO-ANG,TILT — 'Kooter' in, 'Stein' out.
S/D, STICKS — 'Kooter'
S/D, STICKS — 'Bruno'
S/D, STICKS — 'Nug'
S/D, STICKS — 'Kooter'
S/D, STICKS — 'Ty'
S/D, STICKS — 'Stein'
ECU, LOCKED — Prehistoric Porn Magazine

The MASTER/WIDE, from the TILT UP, and 'Kooter's' entrance with the Prehistoric Porn that he will show to 'Bruno', included the entire scene. Notice how low the camera is, about a foot above the water. Also note that 'Stein', 'Ty' and 'Nug' all have eyelines going towards CAMERA RIGHT — they're "watching" 'Grog' (o.s) who is further down the riverbank trying to figure out a solution to the tribe's problem.

Second set-up for the 'Conference' scene by the stream. The camera kept on BABY LEGS and brought closer to the 'line'. A quick lens change for this DIRTY SINGLE of 'Kooter' dreamily offering his "solution" to the 'missing women problem'.

The second DIRTY SINGLE — 'Bruno' looking at the Prehistoric Porn. The camera was brought further into the midst of the group but remains on the 'correct' side of The 180°.

I don't remember exactly, but looking at the height of the lens, we probably panned left from 'Bruno' and kept the same focal length to get this DIRTY SINGLE of 'Nug'. Set-up time? Under a minute.

The next shot, of 'Ty', is also a DIRTY SINGLE. Notice how the height is maintained, and so is the 'size' of the subject in the frame. 'Ty' is looking out of CAMERA RIGHT, maintaining the eyeline that we established earlier in the MASTER.

A change is coming up. The next frame features 'Stein' in his DIRTY SINGLE, but 'Stein' is about to use the tribe's problem to depose 'Grog' as leader and take over. So, we kept the S/D, but we went in closer to get a sense of his growing importance.

Once again, 'Stein's' eyeline is correct, and 'Ty' matches it. Notice that because the focal length has changed to get 'tighter' on 'Stein', the background has been thrown further out of focus than it was in the previous shot. 'Stein' is pin sharp against a very soft-focus b.g., and this helps to increase his prominence in the frame and give us a feeling of his power.

In all these S/D Shots, the camera support barely moved. 4 shots were quickly made by panning the camera and reframing on each actor. With the camera maintaining its position in this way, there was no possibility of 'crossing the line'.

The penultimate shot in the edited sequence takes us back to the MASTER, after 'Stein' has left frame. 'Kooter' is daydreaming and 'Bruno' is still looking at Prehistoric Porn — while 'Ty' and 'Nug' look worriedly towards (o.s.) 'Grog'.

All that remains in this location is to shoot the ECU of the offensive material that has disgusted 'Bruno'...

A loose ECU. It took a moment to get the best frame while not 'crossing the line'. Notice that the shot is not 'Bruno's' direct POV. I wanted the audience to feel that they were sitting beside 'Bruno' and leaning over to get a glimpse. We cheated the shot to the left, so it became more 'Kooter's' POV, even though we know that Kooter's not looking at it. The shot was LOCKED because we added the stick figures in post and didn't want any movement of the frame.

And here's 'Grog' further down the riverbank, attempting to find a solution to the tribe's problem. This shot was made several days after the rest of the scene had been completed. 'Grog' was positioned to Camera Right to maintain a loose sense of the 180° and so that the eyelines we'd previously shot would be believable. There's a mistake, however, in this shot — although, thankfully, it wasn't particularly apparent in the final edit of the film. The camera is too high, too close, and with too 'flat' or 'head-on' an angle — it doesn't give a sense of the POV of the others, particularly 'Stein'. An epic fail on my part! — but life as a director is filled with realizing, too late, what you could have done better.

Every filmmaker will have their own preferred method of Shot Listing. A director I spoke to recently makes index-card sized drawings of each shot in the scene — essentially a storyboard — and pins them up in the production office on a daily basis so everybody can take a look and see which way the wind is blowing. Interestingly, because he has detailed and memorized every shot, this particular director suffers from that Hitchcockian syndrome of feeling that he has made the film before he has actually made the film.

Whatever Shot List methodology you use, the whole point is to 'pre-visualize' your film and make notes that will help you retain that 'vision'. As I keep repeating — use what works for you. I often use a method that puts my Shot List directly into my script. It's a variation on the Lined Script that a Script Supervisor creates as a complete record of the production.

To clarify, a 'Lined Script' is a post-production tool created on-set by your Script Supervisor, in which every shot is fully notated. Not to be confused with a Continuity Script which is a shot-by-shot description of the final delivered film — an important reference for distributors and international translation/foreign dubbing services. (There are a couple of flavors of Continuity Script but let's not get into that now).

To return to the Lined Script. While your Supervisor stands beside you during the entire shoot, they will be recording details of every shot. There's a shorthand to do this — using some of the abbreviations we've already discussed. The notes include a description of shot, lens, action, slate number, dialogue 'covered' and any inconsistencies or errors. Vertical lines drawn in the script indicate how much of the scene was filmed by each shot. The line will continue straight down through dialogue 'on camera' and be drawn as a squiggle thru' dialogue 'off-screen'. All the other notes relating to the shot are listed on the blank page opposite the one being notated. During post-production, if an editor wants to know what shots were made of specific moments — the Lined Script is the 'go-to' source.

As you will immediately see from the example that follows, I've used the 'Lined Script' method to quickly notate the various shots for Scs. 16, 89 and 91.

The first thing to notice is that the shot made first is numbered according to the scene number. The next shot is scene number plus 'A', followed by 'B' and so on. That way I can lay out how I will move through the scene as each Set-Up is reached. This plan may not happen in real-life situations — I could add or delete one of my shots or jump to a shot out of my original sequence order. If so, the Script Supervisor's notes (and by extension the 'Slate' number) will *not* follow my Shot List numbering.

I could, for example, have a certain shot listed as 89A, but on the shoot, I might jump to *my* 89C for the second Set-Up. However, because it's the second Set-Up, the shot will still be listed as 89A on the Slate and the Script Supervisor's Lined Script. In other words, my listing has got nothing to do with the slate number — and everything to do with how I see the series of Set-Ups progressing in my own mind in pre-production.

CONTINUITY STYLE SHOT LISTING

16 *MAS/LS HI-ANG*

TRACK L R

MCU/CU 16A BABY LEGS

16. EXT. ABANDONED SUGAR FACTORY. DAWN.

MS MCU

Jack's BMW appears, tires squealing, and skids to a stop. JACK leaps
out, gun in his hand, runs through a gap in a sagging perimeter fence
and kicks open the door into the building. *MS. W/ PANL-R*

16B   *16C*   *16D REV TRUCK*

89. EXT. ABANDONED SUGAR FACTORY. DAY.

89 LS/MS/2-SHOT - NO FCUS PULL

HELEN's face is bruised and bloodied. She staggers out of the
building, holding onto PIERCE for support. He looks around wildly...

89A S/D MCU   *FCUS*

> PIERCE
>
> Where is he? Where the hell
> is he?!

POV H/H 89B

REV MS-FS P+H ENTER CAM L

HELEN slumps. PIERCE struggles to hold her upright and carry her away
from the building.   *EXIT CAM R*

89C

2-SHOT MCU/EYE   *MS P+H TRACK-R*   *MAS FS*   *FIXED HI-ANG*

PIERCE REACTS

BABY LEGS

91. EXT. ABANDONED SUGAR FACTORY. DAWN.   *LS TRACK W/TRIO*   *FS-MS JACK*

W/JACK

The TRUCK swings off the road at high speed, smashes through the
chain-link fence, sideswipes the dumpsters and skids to a stop. JACK
jumps out and runs to help PIERCE as he half-drags, half-carries HELEN
to safety.

91   *CAM A*   *CAM B*   *91E*
91B   *91C*   *WATCH 180°*   *H/H*

> JACK
>
> What happened?

91D ALL BODY

> PIERCE
>
> Later! We've got to get her
> out of here!

MS MCU   *H/H REV MS MCU*   *WS*   *LOANG MS*

JACK helps PIERCE lift HELEN into the truck. The men climb in after
her, Jack behind the wheel. He slams into gear and the truck takes
off, crashing through another section of the fence. Bouncing crazily
out onto the road, tires screeching, the truck roars away.

91A WATCH 180°   *91F*   *91G*   *PAN L-R*

CAM A CAM B 91H 91S

Notice also that I copy the standard Script Supervisor method of taking a straight line through dialogue that is 'on-camera' and a 'squiggly' line for dialogue that is 'off-camera'.

I really love Shot Listing like this — because it's fast, and it gives me a complete visualization of what I need to do in each scene. However, I never feel constrained to use a single methodology for Shot Listing.

To be perfectly honest, I probably wouldn't use what I call the 'Lined Shot List' methodology for a scene as compli-cated as Sc. 91. It's a great system to use for short, straight-forward scenes like Scs. 16 and 89. I'd probably use the 'Lined' method for part of Sc. 91 — but the full Shot List would be on the left-side facing page to the scene — as would any on-set notes that I'd make during shooting.

On-set, I'd also indicate a preferred 'circled' take num-ber beside the shot, before moving on to the next — and that becomes a further reference for me during the edit.

Well, it's 2019 — or will be in an hour or two and this wraps up *Shooting The List*. I hope it will be of use. Thinking back, I realize I first thought of writing what has become *The Filmmaker's Art* while driving home up Laurel Canyon one evening in 1999. 20 years ago. Life is never instant or direct. Or maybe I'm the King of Procrastination. But I'm glad the series is being published now, rather than earlier. The industry, the technology — all that has changed considerably, and mostly for the better.

Forgive me if my tone has seemed patronizing or 'overly obvious' to you at any time in the three books that make up my views and insights into Development and Pre-Production. It's certainly not a tone, nor an attitude, that I would wish or intend but I am passionate about the filmmaking process and I want to communicate procedures that might seem overtly disci-plined, too traditional, or even unnecessary to current filmmak-ers.

You might think it unnecessary, but I keep finding reasons to hold to my belief in those procedures.

Only today I was on a phone call with a VFX house where a Supervisor was bemoaning the footage that had landed in the suite. The problem? Shots of actors who should have been fitted with prosthetic make-up — but weren't. There had been no preparation in pre-production, so the MUAH Dept were unaware of the requirement. Shooting went ahead anyway, the Director declaring that it would all be 'fixed in post'. You'd think that was the only problem. But the footage was also 'soft'. Not surprising, because if a project is being led sloppily in pre-production, the chances are that principal photography won't be much better. Directors who can't get a grip on their project in pre-production seldom manage to get a grip in production — and end up screaming in post and blaming everyone in sight. In this case, the VFX Supervisor was tasked with adding 'virtual' prosthetic make-up to the faces and bodies of actors who were slightly out of focus. She was trying to decide if the 'virtual' prosthetics should be equally out of focus — knowing she'd be blamed for not being able to 'correct' the bad footage. After a while, I heard a strange banging coming over the phone. It took me a moment to realize that the Supervisor was easing her pain by repeatedly striking her forehead on her desk.

Thus, my insistence on proper preparation.

Finally, I can't leave a 3-book discussion on aspects of Pre-Production without mentioning an issue that gives new and emerging directors considerable difficulty. In fact, this issue is so important that the *Los Angeles Times* once carried an article about a director's struggle to answer the question that he had agonized over for weeks.

- *What do I wear on the shoot? Which of my T-shirts will convey the correct degree of coolness to my crew and colleagues?*

It's probably better to agonize over the script and the casting choices that have been forced on you rather than the message on your T-shirt, but the concern is a real one. I like the Steven Soderbergh look. It's cool, directorial, clean and functional. Grays, blues. Interesting but comfortable footwear. I wish we still lived in an era where a film director could wear a suit and turn up every day looking like a burial plot salesman the way Alfred Hitchcock did. On a number of occasions, I tried to invoke the spirit of Sir Alfred and wore a dark suit, white shirt and tie combo to my shoots. It didn't really work. The crew kept thinking that I was going to leave at any moment to go to a business meeting, so it was very unsettling for them. Plus, you run the risk of looking like one of the Reservoir Dogs and making some sort of slavish, fawning comment on Mr. Tarantino's body of work. I want to be comfortable with the Crew and the Talent, and still be able to walk into a cluster of Executives and not get treated like the hired help. Dressing for directing is really a tough one, let me tell you. Try to plan it well in advance of the shoot. A final word of warning. Don't allow your natural creativity to lead you into doing something weird. This business is uncomfortable with 'weird' when it's standing in their office or on their set.

The last word? Go make a movie. Don't hesitate. The only way to become a filmmaker is to start making films, and the only way to become a great filmmaker is to continue making films until you can no longer be denied.

ABOUT THE AUTHOR

Photo Credit: Hannah Cowley Rath

Markus Innocenti tries not think too much about the sad fact that Orson Welles spent 95% of his professional life trying to fund films and only 5% actually making them. He's directed four feature films, a documentary or two, a handful of commercials and some music videos.
His first screenplay was produced. Which was nice.

ATTRIBUTIONS & ACKNOWLEDGEMENTS

Still frame images from *The Missing Link* used with permission, and with my heartfelt thanks to producers Michael King and Dan Sheldon

The Two-Bit Picture Show Company in association with Something Like Sleep Entertainment presents A Michael King Production A Film by Markus Innocenti *The Missing Link* Screenplay by Michael King, Nicholas King and Dan Sheldon Produced by Michael King and Dan Sheldon. Director of Photography David Lassiter Music Composed by Kevin Saunders Hayes Visual Effects Supervisor Pete Lutke Edited by Markus Innocenti Michael King. Cast K.C. Morgan Leann Slaby Michael King Hillary Novelle Hahn Allen English Mark Mainardi Jenice Marshall Anna Curtis Sean Ridgway Ian Jerrell Chenese Lewis Laura Shields Dan Sheldon Percy Rusty Tiffany Collie Eddie Ruiz. Co-Producer Catherine Shaffer, Associate Producer Jude Fitzmorris, 1st Assistant Director Dan Sheldon, Production Supervisor Jen Warner, Production Coordinator Victoria Perez, 2nd Unit Cinematography Matt Irwin, 1st Assistant Camera Chad Nagel, 2nd Assistant Camera Sean Bagley, Production Sound Mixer Jonathan Lallouz, Gaffer/Key Grip Angelo Soiza, Costume Designer Denise Benton, Key/SFX Make-Up Artist Kathryn Fernandez, Script Supervisor Leigh Miller, Production Assistants German Izquierdo Michael Maguire Casey Norton, Post Production Supervisor Markus Innocenti, 3D Generalist/Rotoscope Artist/ Compositor Peter Lutke, Sound Editor T.A. Moore, Jr., Assistant Sound Editor Sunni Walker, Foley Artist Avis Stanley, ADR Recordist Joel Miller, Additional Music by Colin Campbell, End Credit Music by A Funk Band Named Machete, Media Digitized by The Mission per Jesse Pomeroy, Editorial and Re-Recording Services by Red Dog Logic, Stock Footage provided by POND5, Music Library provided by Jewelbeat, Camera Grip and Lighting provided by Stansbury Studios Inc per Christopher Ross Leong, Shot Entirely on Location in California.

AUTHOR LINKS & FREE DOWNLOADS

https://www.markusinnocenti.com/

Free downloads of material discussed in the books, along with full-color versions of images featured, can be accessed on my website.
Navigate to; Series>The Filmmaker's Art>Media

http://reddoglogic.tumblr.com/

Further pics and info can be found on the Red Dog Logic Tumbler blog.

THE FILMMAKER'S ART SERIES

Currently Available...

Vol 1. DECODING THE SCRIPT
Directors read scripts in ways that others don't, but the Clues are there for everyone to see once they understand how to 'decode'.

Vol 2. SELECTING FOR SUCCESS
Failure to properly prepare for production leads to bad choices and bad films — and sometimes good intentions have unfortunate results.

Vol 3. SHOOTING THE LIST
The Shot List is the Director's roadmap. This book discusses why it is important to have a List, and how to construct one.

Future Volumes... (Titles and Content Not Contractual)

Vol 4. EYE OF A POET
Working with a Director of Photography, understanding basics of Composition, Lighting and Lenses, and the use of Motion and Movement.

Vol 5. ACTORS ON SET
A deep dive into the challenges and rewards of the collaboration between Actors and Directors.

Vol 6. CUTTING FOR KEEPS
Delivering the movie you wanted to make.

Vol 7. MERCHANTS IN THE HOUSE OF FILM
An insider's look at the industry and the career path you might take.

www.ingramcontent.com/pod-product-compliance
Lightning Source LLC
Chambersburg PA
CBHW061728020426

42331CB00006B/1151